I Really Didn't *Want* to Become a Doctor

Tales and Musings from a Retired Family Doc after Over 50-Plus Years of Practice

Howie C. Wolf

Hamilton Books
Lanham • Boulder • New York • Toronto • Plymouth, UK

Copyright © 2017 by
Hamilton Books
4501 Forbes Boulevard
Suite 200
Lanham, Maryland 20706
Hamilton Books Acquisitions Department (301) 459-3366

Unit A, Whitacre Mews, 26-34 Stannary Street,
London SE11 4AB, United Kingdom

Library of Congress Control Number: 2017944837
ISBN: 978-0-7618-6962-7 (pbk : alk. paper)
eISBN: 978-0-7618-6963-4

Dedication

I dedicate this book to my parents, Dr. Henry H. Wolf and Rose Wolf, who made my life and career possible. It is also dedicated to others in my family and the many teachers, professors, colleagues, friends, nurses, and employees who all played integral roles in my life. And, of course, this is for my countless patients who have taught me the most about life itself.

2/14/18

To Ian —

Of all the folks I met through the contacts Marketing" of Wild Rose you are my fave. I don't even know whos in 2nd place!

Hope you enjoy the read and may your days be filled with joy and laughter — Best wishes

Howie

1obb985 @ comcast.

Contents

Foreword

This story is not meant to be an autobiography, but rather a memoir. That's lucky for you, the reader. I merely want to relate to you some background about my experiences in becoming and then being a family doctor. I retired in July 2016 after nearly 54 years of practice, 50 of which were in Boulder County, Colorado. To discuss my personal and family life—my losses and my loves—would add nothing but a distraction from the story I am telling.

Some of you may have read my first book, published with the same title in 2012. But the "tales and musings" have been expanded by a few more years, and I have included additional reflections which relate to my personal doctoring story.

Because of my passion for meaningful health care reform, I have included my take on this subject in the final chapter.

Clinica Family Health Services paid $25 for this book. It would be greatly appreciated if you would send a donation of $25 (or more) to:

Clinica Family Health Services

1345 Plaza Court North

Lafayette, CO 80026

Please signify on check that this donation is in recognition of the book by Howie Wolf

Prologue

At age 25 I found myself, as a rookie Navy doctor, in a boat-swain's chair dangling between two huge ships in the middle of the Pacific Ocean. This "high line" transfer was being done to transport me from the USS Bayfield APA-33 to another troop transport ship to assist a colleague with an appendectomy. My acrophobia—fear

Lt. Wolf on a high-line between two ships.

of heights—and my motion sickness history were adding to the angst already present considering that some such transfers have been known to result in the person in the chair being inadvertently thrust into the sea with its always hungry sharks. I was naturally fearful and pondered: What the fuck am I doing here? If I wasn't a doctor, I would not have been asked to take on this dangerous risk. What's even more significant to consider is this: *I Really Didn't Want to Become a Doctor!*

Early Years

*A*s children of Doc Wolf, my brother Butch, my sister Marcia, and I were expected to lead exemplary lives since we were always under scrutiny by the townspeople, at least according to both our parents. At times I felt constrained by the notion that, as the son of the town's only doctor, I was expected to stay out of trouble. Not surprisingly, many people in the community expected Butch and me to become doctors after leaving Elgin, Iowa. While in high school, Butch worked part time on farms and followed a career path to become a veterinarian. It is widely accepted that to become a doctor one must have a passion for and be proficient in the sciences. What my grammar and high school years revealed was that I preferred literature, writing, math, and music.

A beloved and remarkable man, Dr. Henry Wolf epitomized what was then called a "general practitioner." He delivered babies, set fractures, made house calls, hospitalized patients, and was revered by the community and surrounding towns. Both my parents were from Jewish families in Chicago, and my mother Rose consented to the move to Elgin, Iowa (population 642), when my father was asked in 1930 to replace the

Henry and Rose Wolf, circa 1948.

town's only physician, who had died. Mother was assured that their stay would be no more than five years, but both parents lived out their lives there.

Located in northeast Iowa, Elgin was an idyllic, agricultural town, nestled in a fertile valley. Prominent hills overlooked several rivers and streams that nourished rich, black Iowa soil. The area is aptly nicknamed "Little Switzerland." When I was growing up, the main industry was a corn canning factory, which provided jobs for many people, old and young, as well as a place where local farmers could sell their sweet corn. I worked there as a product inspector's aide during summer breaks from high school. That meant climbing atop the dusty, poorly lit mountains of canned corn cartons to retrieve a sample can for the inspector to taste and document. This was considered a "cushy" job by my pals who worked in the factory and endured more physical labor.

The townsfolk generally leaned toward the conservative side. There were two churches: Methodist and Baptist. And the town always had at least an equal number of bars. Growing up in a place where most people know you can, in some ways, feel protective. If a farmer broke a leg, his neigh-

Butch, Marcia and Howie, circa 1944.

bors would pitch in to do the chores and keep the farm going. But such closeness can also kindle gossip, which can travel quickly through a small town.

Our house was a few hundred yards from the Elgin school, separated by a large barn, barnyard, and hog house. The school housed grades K through 12 and was the hub of Elgin's activities. Our town boasted a downtown and an uptown, barely a mile apart. Located downtown was the gossip center of town, the Coffee Cup Café, which also served as a hangout for kids. My father's office was on the second floor of a downtown office building. The flight of stairs to his office was difficult or impossible for many elderly or disabled patients so my father often made house calls for such patients.

There were only white families in our town. I remember my first experience seeing a black person, a woman so black that she was almost purple. We were visiting relatives in Chicago, and I was about four years old. My mother sensed my confusion and explained that not everyone had white skin. But her words implied that the character of a person should never be based on skin color.

But I really revolted against becoming a doctor because of what I saw in my father's daily life. He would get called out at night to deliver a baby, give an anesthetic (ether at that time) for a surgeon, or tend to other urgent medical problems. I remember a farmer dropping by our house during a Sunday family dinner with a severe, gory arm injury from a threshing machine, so Doc Wolf met the man at the office. As teenagers, my siblings and I complained when some insensitive woman decided to go into labor just when we were set to go on a vacation to Clear Lake! His vocation deprived his own kids of important beach time! So when people in Elgin would ask me, then a high school student, if I was going to become a doctor like my father, I had a standard, smart-aleck response: *Why would anyone want to go to school for that many years just to have his meals, sleep, and vacations interrupted by needy patients?*

Education:
College & Medical School

*I*n September 1952, having just graduated from Elgin High School, I decided to attend the University of Iowa in Iowa City. There I thoroughly enjoyed the philosophy, history, literature, and psychology courses. My math passion dwindled when my trigonometry professor gave me a well-deserved "D" for the course.

Campus life in the early 1950s reflected the cautious post-World War II era. Politically, Iowa City was on the map. Dwight "Ike" Eisenhower made a campaign speech from the back of a train in Iowa City. Interest in elections and national affairs was keen. There were regular arguments between Adlai Stevenson and Ike supporters on campus and in the dorms. Although the Montgomery Bus Boycott featuring activist Rosa Parks did not occur until 1955, we heard the rumblings of unrest and violence toward Negroes, especially in the South. Negroes. That's what African Americans were called then. It was a term of both common use and derision. I found myself always siding with the oppressed and could never understand why one human being would mistreat another just because of skin color. An avid baseball fan, I was pleased when Jackie Robinson broke into the Major Leagues and played with the Brooklyn Dodgers in the late 1940s and 1950s. I was fortunate to have seen this amazing athlete play several times at Wrigley Field. I was aware when other baseball teams acquired Negro players and could not understand why they were not allowed to play during the years before.

I had many friends during my freshman year at The Quadrangle, the main dorm. Unlike Elgin there was a wide diversity of races represented in my classes and at The Quad. Among my friends was Hank Berry, a Negro from Chicago who played for the Iowa Hawkeyes baseball team. Except for my father's Negro roommate in a tuberculosis sanatorium a few years earlier, a soft-spoken man named Mr. Cotton, Hank was the first black person with whom I had conversed. He was a handsome, athletic, bright young man with a big smile and sensitivity for the civil rights struggles going on. Skin color didn't matter to either of us in this college friendship.

One day we were in downtown Iowa City, and Hank said he needed a haircut and had to get back to the dorm before the barber shop there closed. I asked why he didn't just get his haircut downtown. I even offered to introduce him to my barber just around the corner. Hank said, "Oh, no, Howie, the downtown barbers won't cut our hair. They say they don't have the training." That just did not sound right to me, and my activist social justice gene was about to express itself! I helped organize a group of like-minded people and, over a period of several months, city council meetings, and a lot of nasty letters to the editor at *The Daily Iowan* — representing both sides of the issue — we prevailed. The barber shops in Iowa City were finally open to all races and in 1953 this was a major deal. The only downside for me was that Bill, the barber I'd been using since starting my freshman year, asked me to find another barber. He knew I had been connected with the protests.

Many fellow students avoided interacting with people of other races, but I seemed to be drawn to them. The social injustices of that era were obvious and revolting to me. During a driving trip in the Deep South with high school buddies two years earlier, I witnessed overt racism. The "Whites Only" and "Negroes Only" signs were ubiquitous while traveling through Louisiana, Mississippi, Alabama, and Florida. Such discrimination based on skin color always seemed cruel and simply wrong.

In June 1953 as my freshman year ended, a college pal, Dick Wisott, invited me to his family's home in Sioux City for a long weekend. The Monday morning that we were to leave to go back to Iowa City, a friend of Dick's called and asked for our help at his father's turkey farm adjacent to the Floyd River, a big tributary to the Missouri River. It had been raining for several days and a flood crest was expected in the Floyd River in mid-afternoon. But in the late morning, as we were loading crates of turkeys onto a truck, we could see the six-foot-tall, ominous crest of water rapidly coming toward us! It was frightening. Within minutes, just like in the newsreels we've all seen, our crew was atop the turkey dwelling wondering if we would be rescued! My heart raced as screaming voices—cries for help—could be heard in nearby houses and trailer parks. A small motorboat eventually came by to bring us to safety. The Floyd River flood of 1953 claimed fourteen lives, including three children.

During my sophomore year, I joined a Jewish fraternity perhaps because I felt I needed some real Jewish exposure, having had little in Elgin. Dick Wisott was my fraternity brother, and, with other frat renegades, we did some rather fun and crazy things. Perhaps the most memorable was when we wadded up single sheets of newspapers and completely filled the room of an annoying brother who was out of town for the weekend. Even his door could not be easily opened because of our clever newspaper blockade. Of course, brother Alan was aggravated when he returned and tried to enter his room. But he figured correctly that the dastardly deed was probably done by Dick, Howie, and Harvey, another one of our fellow conspirators.

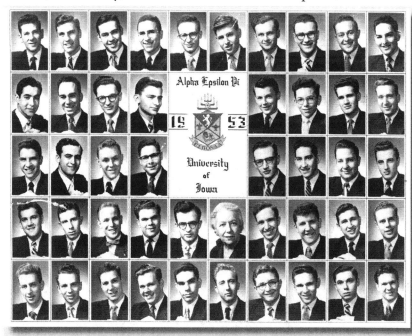

Howie Wolf (fourth row, third from left)
Dick Wisott (fourth row, second from right)
Jerry Silberman (Gene Wilder – fifth row, sixth from left)

There was an interesting freshman student who had just joined AEPi. Jerry Silberman was from Milwaukee and came to the University of Iowa to study acting. I did not know him well or "hang with him" but he was always an energetic and funny guy. Jerry went on to become the famous actor Gene Wilder, whose talented career is widely known. His memorable roles in *Willie Wonka's Chocolate Factory* and *Young Frankenstein* received world wide acclaim. Gene Wilder died in August 2016 at the age of 83.

The State University of Iowa made national and even world news in 1955 when the selection of "Miss State University of Iowa" was revealed. The event focused on beauty and talent and the winner was selected from many candidates representing the dormitories and sororities. The surprise winner was 17-year-old Dora Martin, a Negro freshman from Houston, who sang "The Yellow Rose of Texas" for her talent. I remember the event, and how it evoked various reactions from my fellow students. Some like me were pleased that skin color was not being used to judge a person's beauty and talent. Others expressed an unsettling feeling that even our Midwestern university could harbor expressions of the civil rights movement which they feared.

But the university officials silently limited and even cancelled Dora's public appearances to limit her exposure. However, 60-plus

Dora Martin was crowned Miss SUI.

years later, in 2016, the University of Iowa publicly apologized to Dora Martin Berry. The University held programs that fall titled "Fields of Opportunity: UI's Black Migration Stories," where Dora spoke at a panel of the complex dynamics of race in the middle of the last century. University President Bruce Harreld went to the podium and apologized to Dora for the university's shameful behavior. He acknowledged that during her reign in 1955 she had represented the school with "pride, dignity, and grace." He and Dora shed tears as his words came forth. Dora is now a social worker in New Jersey and an active member of the Iowa Black Alumni Association. Coincidentally, she married my Negro college friend, Henry (Hank) Berry, who played baseball for the University of Iowa and experienced discrimination regularly when the team was on the road for away games. When the University of Iowa baseball team was on the road, Henry had to share a room with the bus driver instead of with his teammates.

As my sophomore year ended, I still had no inkling regarding a career and kept dwelling about my personal mantra: *Choose any profession other than medicine.*

I came home to Elgin for the summer and worked a construction job. That gave me time to ponder my father's vocation and wonder why he was so enamored of being a doctor. I started paying more

Howie joined the Medical Student Council at the University of Iowa College of Medicine in 1957 (middle row, first from left).

attention to him and his work and sensed the gratification he received from helping his patients.

Dr. Henry Wolf treated all patients, whether rich or poor, with dignity and respect. Money and insurance were not issues back then when an office call was $3.00 and a house call was $5.00. His fee for total OB care was $135.00 which included all prenatal care, delivery, 6-week checkup, and care of the baby. Yet many patients in our agricultural community paid Doc's bills with all sorts of products from homemade sausage to sides of pork or beef. A local mason owed dad a rather large sum because of expenses incurred by a family member's serious illness. Mr. Boleyn's payment came in the form of the biggest and best backyard brick barbeque grill in Elgin. When patients couldn't pay, Dad treated them anyway.

Merriam-Webster's definition of *epiphany* is "a sudden, striking understanding of something." Perhaps it was that I paid more attention to my father's dedication and interaction with patients. Maybe after some time at college and away from home, my awareness of what it might be like to be a doctor was heightened.

Medicine offered a career in intellectual challenges while providing service to patients. Financial security was part of the lure as well. Clearly, my father was highly respected by his patients, colleagues, friends, and family. I was finally starting to "get it" that the gratification my father received trumped the long years of education, irregular hours, patients' needs, and cancelled vacations. It must have been after one of those epiphany moments that I announced to my father that in my upcoming third

Howie helping to provide hydration to fellow medical student David Taft on the way to 1958 Rose Bowl.

year of college I was going to take basic pre-med courses like biology and chemistry and was considering medicine as a career. Rather than receiving the news with joy and pride — as I had hoped and expected — his expression was a scowl. "Choosing medicine as a career, Howie," he said, "is not like choosing a different car or a new girlfriend! Medicine requires a lifetime of dedication and continuous study."

With some trepidation, I accepted the challenge, registered for the needed courses that fall, and surprisingly received quite good grades. The next spring I applied for medical school, passed the interview process and was accepted to the University of Iowa College of Medicine in 1955. My feelings of insecurity and confusion over career choice were, for now, improved. Even during the first two years of medical school, I was not passionate about science courses, especially biochemistry. But during the third and fourth years, I was fairly sure that I had made the right choice. Direct contact with patients and the challenges of assessing symptoms and signs plus learning diagnostic skills convinced me that I was in the right place.

It was in the exam room, when I was finally seeing patients, that I learned the importance of the most basic medical skills: how to obtain a medical history and perform a physical exam. The information obtained during a history and physical exam can point toward a diagnosis, sometimes quickly and without the aid of imaging studies! I felt comfortable with these parts of becoming a doctor, knowing this was what I would be doing later in life.

Medical school was not just about learning to become a doctor but also learning to study very hard to avoid being one of the 20% who dropped out or flunked out. Being an average student, I had to spend more hours hitting the books than some of my gifted classmates. They could go on dates, party, and then cram the night before a big exam and get better grades than me! How I envied them! Later, however, I realized that this hard work gave me a genuine appreciation of the profession. I observed that not all medical students or doctors, even those with straight A's, were comfortable talking with patients. Perhaps my small-town upbringing gave me an advantage in this respect.

Hospitals and teaching institutions are not necessarily the sterile and grave places you might expect. Laughter is indeed good medicine, and we saw plenty administered during medical school. One morning during physical diagnosis class, a surgery professor was demonstrating that in a male patient with an inguinal hernia, listening with a stethoscope over the scrotum could reveal bowel sounds — proving that a part of his intestine had become part of the hernia sac. Such a finding could, therefore, rule out the more serious masses sometimes contained in the scrotum. We all dutifully held our stethoscopes over the scrotums of the blue-and-white-striped robed men in the unit. Just then, fellow student Kelly, who was notoriously late for classes and sessions such as these, arrived and was struck by the strange scene. The professor asked Kelly to auscultate (listen with a stethoscope) a patient's scrotum. When asked what he heard, Kelly — totally uninformed about the diagnostic mission — sheepishly turned to the professor and guessed: *"Normal testicular sounds?"*

When I was a third-year medical student on the urology service, I heard several patients who had recently undergone prostate surgery talking about playing a game of Rummy. However, there was an obvious problem. Each man had a catheter draining his bladder and each had to carry around a two-gallon jug to collect the urine, which nurses were required to monitor for volume and signs of blood or infection. As these geezers were trying to figure out a solution, I realized I had a lecture to attend, so I left. When I returned, the scene I saw before me was classic Norman Rockwell: four old men clad in the hospital issued blue-and-white-striped robes, each with his catheter draining into a single shared jug beneath the card table! The nurses were certainly unable to accurately assess the amount or clarity of each man's urinary output, but those guys gleefully enjoyed their game of Rummy and were probably better for it.

Internship

*A*fter graduating with a doctorate in medicine in 1959, I chose to intern at John Sealy Hospital, a University of Texas Medical Branch facility in Galveston. This institution had a favorable reputation for teaching and provided a rotating internship where the intern spent time learning his trade in various departments such as internal medicine, pediatrics, obstetrics, and surgery. What really influenced my decision to intern there, however, was the fact that the hospital was still segregated. Except for pediatrics, white patients and black patients had separate wards and facilities.

My activist self had only been temporarily put on hold during medical school. Part of me wanted to see firsthand why it was that separation of the races was the norm in the South. I wanted to see how I would respond to a real-life situation, instead of carrying the possible false impressions obtained in college. Living in multicultural and multiracial Iowa City, racial prejudice was not overt. I needed to see for myself if the frequent racist remarks I had heard in the Midwest, from young and old, had validity in the Deep South. After all, I had known and befriended only a few "college Negroes" in Iowa City and perhaps a closer look at folks in Galveston would change my non-prejudiced attitude.

Most of my fellow interns and residents were from Southern medical schools, and all were white males. Many clung tenaciously to their stereotypical, racist views. I found that, in the main, my black patients were friendlier and more appreciative than whites for the care they received in this charity hospital. Degrading comments to black and Hispanic patients from doctors and nurses were not uncommon, so being treated with dignity and respect by a white doctor was unusual but appreciated. I will never forget a little black woman, dying of cancer, who particularly appreciated my caring attitude and, with a smile on her face, she instructed her daughter bring me from their home a basket of Southern fried chicken. Like the home-made or homegrown payments that my father had received, this gift of fried chicken was simple but came straight from the heart. The lessons I had learned from my parents about not being judgemental of a person's character based on race or financial status gave me a solid foundation for my internship.

While in Galveston, I met and worked with a black X-ray technician, Clarice Davis, who became a lifelong friend. Black. That was the new replacement term for "Negro." Our relationship was inexplicable in the many ways our lives ran parallel courses through the years.

Clarice and I saw each other often during my internship, since most services that were part of my rotation — surgery, internal medicine, pediatrics, even OB — required the doctor to go the X-ray department. Frequently Clarice would be there and, if we had time, we would slip over to the cafeteria and talk over coffee. As I got to know him, I realized that my instincts had not betrayed me. Like Mr. Cotton and Hank Berry, Clarice Davis had dark skin. However, the three men were different human beings who came from different places and often had varying views. Amazingly, much like any three white men!

Clarice and I made a pact to stay in touch with one another after my internship ended. We exchanged holiday cards, but mostly we called each other at random times throughout the years. Near the 15-year mark of our friendship, he told me that he and his wife were divorcing and that it might cause a few issues with his three children. Coincidentally, I had three kids and was going through a divorce nearly at the same time. In July 1981, after one year of marriage, my second wife, Jonni Scott, was killed in a gruesome car accident in Boulder. At about the same time, Clarice's second wife was killed in a boating accident! In the late 1980s, Clarice called me and asked how I was and how my kids were. After I told him everyone was fine, he revealed that his oldest son had taken his own life. Not many years later — in January of 1991 — my oldest son Jeff took his own life. This extraordinary bond between Clarice and me has continued despite these setbacks. We seem to look at things the same way in terms of social justice and politics. And then there was a time in the early

1990s when I was dating a black nurse at the same time that he was dating a Jewish divorcee....

Looking back, I probably encountered more Hispanic patients than blacks during my internship. I developed a deep appreciation for their culture and language. Without trying to stereotype, it seemed to me that most Latinos appreciated what they had in life—not material possessions but extremely tight family connections not customarily seen among whites. I often saw dozens of relatives — some close and some not so close — visiting a sick Hispanic family member in the hospital. White patients rarely had so many visitors. Learning to understand and speak a little español became one of my biggest challenges. Trying to obtain a patient's medical history and do a physical exam through an interpreter is not the same as being able to communicate directly.

As a Midwesterner and graduate of the University of Iowa College of Medicine, I began my internship feeling insecure and unsure whether I really had the right stuff to be a real doctor. Further, I was unfamiliar with Southern customs and colloquialisms. During my emergency room rotation late one night, amidst other varied cases, a large and loud woman's screams could be heard in the corridors. "I'ze got a risin' in mah ear, I'ze got a risin' in mah ear!" she shouted. A nurse and I finally calmed her enough for me to place my otoscope into her ear. I thought she'd be pleased when I announced reassuringly, "Ma'am, there's no raisin in your ear. It must have come out." She was not happy, however, and shrieked straight away that she had a risin' and not a raisin in her ear. The nurse explained that in the South a "risin'" means swelling or "rising." I felt chagrined when I looked more closely at the edge of the patient's ear canal and saw what appeared to be a tiny boil.

In a way, this was like a continental language barrier. As a Yankee, I had not encountered many of the Southern words and customs. The ER nurse served much like an interpreter for me — in our own country with a fellow English speaker.

Because Galveston is on the Gulf of Mexico, the emergency room yielded some unique conditions. I saw many patients with severe skin rashes caused by jellyfish, but the most dramatic injuries were caused by stingrays whose barbs could be lethal. One young man I saw required surgery because a stingray had caused a penetrating abdominal injury.

As they had their own colloquialisms, some people in Texas had their own health care traditions that I could not have imagined. When I was on the pediatric service, I saw a two-week-old baby die of neonatal tetanus because it was customary in some poor rural areas to cover a newborn's cut umbilical cord with cow dung. The pediatrics wards were in stark, strange contrast to the segregation in the adult wards. Children of all backgrounds and races ate and played happily together. They understood at their young age what their parents might never grasp.

One day while making rounds on patients in the internal medicine wards, I had written some orders and spoken to the nurses and student nurses about patients under my care. As I walked away, I heard a collective giggle come from the group. Had I written an inappropriate, laughable order? Did they think that I was stupid? I turned on the spot and asked, "Did I write a wrong order or what?" A student nurse volunteered with her thick Southern accent, "Oh, no sah, Dr. Wolf, it's jus' that y'all talk so funny!"

Sickness and surgery knew no hours, so interns and residents were frequently on call, sometimes pulling "all-nighters" and then seeing clinic patients the next day. The only bright spot about being on call was the syrupy, sexy voice of Barbara, the night switchboard operator for John Sealy Hospital. In the middle of the night, Barbara's voice would awaken the on-call doctor with her thick Southern accent: "Oh, Doctah Wolf, sorry 'bout disturbin' y'all at this hour, darlin', but the gals over on Four North need y'all to drop by right soon cuz some patient is havin' problems breathin.'"

Neither I nor any of my fellow interns and residents had ever seen Barbara. But we fanaticized that she must be about 24 and look like a *Playboy* centerfold. Her sexy, man-magnet voice was impossible to ignore. One night when I was on call for obstetrics, Barbara's phone call awakened me with, "Oh, Doctah Wolf, so sorry to botha' y'all, but ah'm sooo excited! Y'all's on OB call an' mah' daughter Amy is 'bout to have mah' firs' gran'chile, and y'all will be the one to deliver her!"

My fantasies were dashed. Surely she had to be 35 or 40 years old to be a grandmother! As I hurried to the OB ward, I clung to the hope that Barbara would possess breathtaking beauty however "old" she might be. I arrived on the labor and delivery deck and finally laid eyes on our fantasy operator. Barbara was probably one of the ugliest women I'd ever seen: bad hair, bad body, and bad teeth. I'll not go on. But she was also a warm and genuinely friendly person who beamed when I handed to her a precious, new granddaughter!

When I told one of my closest intern friends Bud Price the truth about Barbara, I could sense his disillusionment and disappointment. I asked him his thoughts about telling the rest of the guys. "Hell, no," he said. "Let 'em keep having their stupid fantasy!" But that syrupy, nighttime voice was never the same for me.

United States Navy

*A*fter finishing my internship on June 30, 1960, I wasn't sure about specializing. I had considered applying for either a pediatric or psychiatry residency program in Galveston. Family practice residency programs did not exist then. I never had much personal interest in the military. Perhaps the feeling came from knowing that rank matters, and I obviously do not like the notion of subordinating people for any reason. I had played trombone in the University of Iowa Marching Band mainly because that was the only legitimate way to avoid mandatory ROTC (Reserve Officers Training Corps) required for all male students. It was not that I possessed great musical talent!

But doctors were being drafted, and I didn't want to start a practice somewhere only to be taken into the Army a few months or years later. I decided to be a Navy doctor. I had read about the duties and expectations of that position and favored the notion of becoming a Navy doctor rather than enlisting in the Army or Air Force. What a Navy doctor might do seemed closer to general practice than working in a battalion aid station or being a flight surgeon.

Our country was abuzz worrying about the Communist threat in Southeast Asia and what we should do about it. The Kennedy-Nixon debates covered these concerns but barely touched on the civil rights issues soon to come to the fore in the mid-1960s. Despite my personal feelings about military and war, I am glad that our country is strong militarily and have the utmost respect for those who have served. I was not in favor of invading Southeast Asia but suspected such U.S. action would become inevitable. On the civil rights scene, in 1960 the well-known lunch counter sit-ins began in Greensboro, North Carolina. The brave black people who crossed that line were an inspiration to many others who followed their lead at other lunch counters and restaurants in other Southern states.

On July 11, 1960, I began my first Navy duty assignment in Oakland at Oak Knoll Naval Hospital. During this two-week stint,

I learned how, when, and to whom one must salute and which uniform to wear when and where. I was then assigned to an amphibious ship, the USS Bayfield APA-33, a troop transport home-based in San Diego.

To be a ship's only doctor for 800 to 1500 men was a definite challenge and a huge responsibility. Were it not for the daily guidance and suggestions from my chief hospital corpsman Chief O'Connor, I could not have figured out the Navy ship doctor's role. Of course, this was my first experience practicing medicine where there was no one to call for help. Many of my shipmates — officers and enlisted men alike — thought that I really longed to practice my rookie medical skills on them. Some even suggested that my biggest desire would be to perform operations at sea to gain experience I'd eventually need in private practice. They were wrong! The last thing I wanted was the onus of doing surgery in the tiny surgical room down in sick bay with its limited supplies and the lack of an anesthesiologist or a surgical assistant! I knew I would not be comfortable doing such surgery, especially open abdominal surgery, in that tiny room. I also knew that there would be no one around to help if I got into trouble. It was not useful or funny when the ship's jovial dentist, Lt. Fred Martinez, offered to administer nitrous oxide on a surgical patient should the need arise. While that substance, also known as laughing gas, might help with a dental procedure, it would probably be of little help with an emergency appendectomy. Chief O'Connor knew the whereabouts of the surgical and medical supplies within that tiny operating room. That was somewhat reassuring!

My closest friends aboard the Bayfield were the medical corpsmen with whom I worked every day. I had less in common with my fellow officers. Many seemed arrogant and overly impressed with how they outranked the lowly enlisted men. Like me, the corpsmen were more committed to taking care of the sick and injured than worrying about whether the engine room boiler was functioning or what the captain was doing. Although some were better trained than others, all were hard workers who helped our medical department run quite efficiently. Being the only medical officer, I felt responsible to help with the training of our corpsmen so we had regular sessions to learn about diseases and treatment.

Tony, one of my corpsmen, had grown up in Honolulu. So when our ship had a stop in Hawaii, our whole medical department accepted his invitation to show us Oahu. He not only gave us a tour of the luxurious island, but his mother insisted he invite us to their hillside Honolulu home for dinner. What a beautiful evening it was! The colorful sunset illuminated the ocean, but the subsequent bright moon and thousands of stars allowed the lush view to continue. Tony's mother was replete with warm hospitality and pride in the Hawaiian culture to enhance our enjoyment. She fed us fresh fruit, delicious roasted pig, and many scrumptious trimmings. I even tried poi for the first and last time. By the end of the evening, I felt that our medical department was more like a bunch of friends than a bunch of military guys with different ranks enjoying good food and good times while appreciating this fascinating culture.

When we returned to the ship, however, I was chastised by the Executive Officer (XO) for "fraternizing with enlisted men." I had already resented many features of the military caste system, but when this officer, second in command to the Captain, told me who my friends should be, on the ship or ashore, I was angry. My activist gene was stirring again. I really wanted to point out that, although the XO outranked me, his concerns about what I did ashore were inappropriate as long as I didn't do anything illegal. We may have different stripes designating our ranks, but we are still human beings, not better than someone else because we outrank them. Would he rather I hang out with that obnoxious, grown-up-brat ensign freshly graduated from Brown University whose greatest pleasure seemed to be ordering sailors in his unit to do unpleasant tasks? Not wanting to risk a court-martial charge, I kept my mouth shut.

In the spring of 1961, when our ship set sail from Hawaii, it was quite disturbing to notice we were not heading east back to California. Instead, the USS Bayfield was loaded with marines and was heading west. We learned that President Kennedy had ordered our amphibious squadron of eight ships, along with air support, to invade Laos to help squelch the Communist takeover of Southeast Asia. Sure, I had joined the Navy knowing that sometimes war happens, but my personal, selfish mission was to get my two years of active duty out of the way so I could go practice medicine somewhere. Being a troop transport, the USS Bayfield took on about 1200 marines ready to do battle if needed. Most of my shipmates displayed no visible angst over the possible invasion with its inherent dangers. We knew little of the mood of the country regarding the possibility of war since all the news came from the high-ranking Bayfield officers.

Most of the sailors and marines aboard had not yet received immunizations needed for that area. I had studied yellow fever and cholera in medical school, but I never anticipated I might be immunizing people against those diseases or even seeing patients suffering from them. I was not well informed regarding the treatment of those or any other tropical diseases I might be seeing. Remember this was 30 years before the internet was available.

The admiral of the squadron happened to be riding aboard our ship so we were therefore deemed the flagship. Unbeknownst to most of us while in Hawaii, the Bayfield was stocked with vaccines for yellow fever and many other tropical diseases. Of course, material for possible major battles was put on board all squadron ships. The vaccines had to be distributed to the other seven ships while traversing the Pacific. One by one, the other ships came close to the Bayfield to receive their allotment of vaccines for their corpsmen to administer to their shipmates. This was accomplished by a "high-line transfer," a series of pulleys and ropes (lines) between the two ships. It was an amazing feat for this young sailor to observe.

With the admiral aboard, I was the designated chief medical officer in all the military sessions including plans to set up battalion aid stations after hitting the beach in Laos. Although I was frightened by the notion of going to a strange place and seeing horrible injuries and tropical diseases, I was resigned just to go with the flow. Truthfully, I had no choice but to try to do my best.

But when we arrived in Okinawa, the plans had mercifully changed, and our squadron of ships was ordered by the commander of all Pacific forces to go back to Hawaii within a few days. I was so glad that we were not going to war. Most of my shipmates were relieved, too. Many of us hit the beach (went to bars) in Okinawa to celebrate, but I do not have a clear memory of those evenings!

Two days into the return trip, a fellow medical officer, Dr. Paulson on a sister ship, notified the Bayfield captain via ship's phone that he had diagnosed appendicitis in one of his men and requested permission for me to be high-lined to his ship to assist at surgery.

It was a clear day and the sea was calm as the two vessels came side by side. I took a razzing from my fellow officers about how such transfers had often landed the passenger in the "drink," also known as the shark-infested ocean. I was reassured, however, by the chief boatswain. He told me that, after getting into the cage for the transfer, I shouldn't be afraid. The chief said, "Doc, don't look down, don't look back at the Bayfield and don't look at the ship you're being sent to. Just look up [toward heaven?], and you'll be fine."

I did look up as the chief suggested. But looking up at that little chair dangling precariously amidst pulleys and lines, I was reminded of how frightened, sick, and embarrassed I had been on a Ferris wheel ride as a teenager with my date. I had become pale, sweaty, and very nauseated on a ride considered by most to be rather wimpy. What the chief didn't know is that *I Really Didn't Want to Become a Doctor!*

The transfer indeed was carried out without incident, and within an hour I was helping a colleague perform a successful appendectomy. I thought the powers that be would allow me to ride the rest of the way to Hawaii on Dr. Paulson's ship. But the very next day Chief O'Connor on the Bayfield called the captain of the ship I was on and said he thought one of our sailors had also developed appendicitis. He requested that Lt. Wolf return immediately to assess the situation and operate if necessary.

The return trip high-line transfer did not frighten me so much since I had breezed through the first one without incident. However, I should have paid closer attention to the different situations. This time the sea was rough, the waves were higher, the wind was howling, and the ships had difficulty achieving side-to-side positioning. Consequently, the ride back was very scary as I was bounced up and down and from side to side in my little chair cage. Upon my arrival back on the USS Bayfield, the chief boatswain told me that if they had sent me a minute sooner or a minute later, I would have been dropped into the drink!

I agreed with Chief O'Connor's diagnosis, so I did perform my first and last solo appendectomy at sea. It was a memorable event, even worse than I had imagined. The tiny surgical room was barely large enough to hold the patient and his nervous surgeon, plus a couple of corpsmen including the chief. There was no general anesthesia available, so I chose to administer a spinal anesthetic. The sterile, powdered pontocaine had to be mixed with a sterile diluent just before administering. The ship was rocking noticeably throughout the whole operation. Luckily, I got into the spinal canal with ease and slowly injected the pontocaine solution. After the injection, we tilted the table a bit downward to ensure that the patient's lower body would become anesthetized. Then we waited. And we waited some more. Testing the patient's skin sensation with a pin prick, the legs and lower abdomen were becoming numb — but not very numb. His abdominal muscles were not relaxed and he was still far too sensitive on the skin of his abdomen. Before the weak anesthetic wore off, I had to act.

I was overwhelmed with the situation at hand. I was nervous but did not display my internal fears. A man's life was in my hands. If I screwed up, I had nowhere to turn, no one to ask for help. I administered some Demerol and figured that even a little nitrous oxide given by the quirky shipboard dentist, Lt. Fred Martinez, might ease the patient's discomfort. It worked. With the chief corpsman as my assistant, I was able to do the appendectomy—a procedure I had only witnessed during internship days. The post-op period was uneventful, but I asked the chief what might have been wrong with the anesthetic.

It turns out that, per Navy regulations, all material in the surgery rooms must be sterilized every three months. My suspicion is that the pontocaine powder had been sterilized so many times that its effectiveness had diminished. Happily, the patient survived despite the inadequate anesthesia, limited equipment, and the extremely nervous surgeon.

Big ships have cockroaches. They are ubiquitous. Ask any sailor. But the ship's medical officer must assume the role of public health officer. I learned quickly that cockroaches and other vermin would not be tolerated, especially by the captain and other high-ranking officers. One night at 2:00 am, I was awakened by the captain's steward because Capt. Anderson had seen a cockroach racing about in the officers' dining room! Of course the ship received regular anti-varmint spray downs, no doubt putting bad chemicals into the air. The cockroaches could be controlled but not eliminated, and I never did understand why the captain insisted on having me awakened at such an early hour. Perhaps it was simply the joy of ordering a junior officer around, with utter disregard for interrupting someone's sleep.

My second year as a Navy doctor was spent at the Naval Station Dispensary in Long Beach. Those readers old enough to remember the late actor Jackie Cooper's *Hennesey* series on television (it ran from 1959 to 1962) might recognize this facility as the site used for the filming. I worked in the department that saw only males: active duty men, retired Navy men, and dependent sons. The active duty men were always seen first each morning and afternoon for "Sick Call." Here I had to hone my skills at differentiating the truly sick and injured from the malingerers. A large percentage of patients complained of back pain, and quite a few were seen because of the worry they had contracted a sexually transmitted disease.

Thousands of retired Navy men and dependent sons in the Long Beach area were eligible for health care at the Naval Station Dispensary. To ensure that our clinic ran efficiently, we set up an appointment system to accommodate patients needing to be seen soon for illnesses or injuries and those who wanted to schedule future physical exams. One day, however, a retired captain came to our section demanding that he receive a physical exam that day. He did not have or even want an appointment. When told he could be given a time to return for a complete physical exam the following week, he stormed down the hall to speak to my commanding officer, a career Navy doctor named Captain Zuska. Minutes later the two of them marched stridently toward my office where I was ordered to do a physical on the retired captain right then. My resentment for this caste system increased that day. Why should a retired captain or any officer be granted privileges ahead of a retired enlisted man? I do feel that pulling rank in the military mimics other types of social injustices. Of course, I recognize that the higher-ranking individuals must see to it that many orders are carried out properly and with haste. So I'm not against the military hierarchy per se but, in my view, to dehumanize or put down a person because of lower rank in many circumstances is a just a glorified, legal form of bullying.

My Navy career ended on June 30, 1962. I had enjoyed some exciting experiences and learned a lot while in the Navy but definitely did not want to become a career military physician! I checked ads in various state medical journals and decided to accept an offer from the Longmont Clinic in Colorado, a multispecialty group looking for another family doctor. My sister Marcia and her family had settled in the Denver area a year or so earlier and loved the milder-than-Iowa winter weather and majestic mountains. Because I had to take and pass Colorado's Basic Science and Medical Licensure exams, I was not able to start in Longmont until September.

I accepted my father's invitation to practice with him in Elgin, Iowa, for those few months. My experience there again revealed how I had come to idolize my father and his work. Working there as a doctor with people who knew me as a kid growing up made for some memorable and uncomfortable times. One evening, my dad asked me to meet a patient at the office. The patient, a toddler with an earache, was the daughter of Earl, one of my high school classmates. As I was examining the little girl, Earl glared at me with a look I'll never forget. That look told me he was questioning my ability to "doctor his child" since I was the same guy with whom he had played football and performed some daring teenage Halloween pranks. Even more embarrassing was when my father asked if I wanted to listen to the heart of a patient with an interesting heart murmur caused by rheumatic fever. The patient happened to be my very dignified high school English teacher. I blushed sheepishly as my stethoscope touched her bared chest. Mrs. Schori was not at all rattled, but I most certainly was!

Private Practice Begins
in Longmont

I began practicing at the Longmont Clinic in September 1962. This facility had a lab, X-ray facilities, a surgical room, and eleven specialists covering the areas of orthopedics, surgery, urology, internal medicine, and EENT (eye, ear, nose, and throat). I was the second family doctor and, between the two of us, we took care of a large number of pediatric and obstetric patients. Besides our full clinic days, we made house calls, cared for our hospitalized patients, delivered babies, and did some surgical assisting.

Then, Longmont was a growing town of just over 12,000 people. The sugar factory was the main industry and a turkey processing plant, built later, was a close second. By the end of the decade, both the Federal Aviation Administration and IBM had built facilities in the area, adding significantly to Longmont's employment prospects. I was active in the Junior Chamber of Commerce and served as a Director on the Board of the Longmont Chamber of Commerce as the town continued to attract new industry and grow. When I left Longmont at the end of 1973, the population was near 50,000.

Of course, national issues impacted our small town. The Vietnam War's first combat mission was in 1962 and several of my patients served in that war. A bright, young patient of mine was killed at age 22, probably one of the first Longmont casualties. I saw the devastation the loss caused to his family and friends.

The Civil Rights Act passed in 1964. Longmont's history included discrimination against Hispanics exemplified by "No Mexicans Allowed" signs in some store windows. There were very few blacks living in Longmont, and it is widely known that blacks had difficulty buying houses in Boulder, as well as Longmont. During my 11-year stint at the Longmont Clinic, I had quite a few Hispanic patients, several Japanese American families, but no blacks. It was not unusual to hear anti-black or anti-Mexican epithets at social gatherings during those years.

It was far easier to be a physician in a private group practice than to be a Navy doctor. Certainly, our meetings were more democratic than those experienced in the military. At least one could express views without fear of being court-martialed!

There were no emergency room docs in those days, so all family doctors, internists, and surgeons were required to take turns covering Longmont United Hospital's emergency room. We would be on call for a week at a time and often extremely busy with severely sick and injured patients. I recall a particularly gruesome motorcycle accident where two bikes, each carrying a passenger, collided. Only two of the four survived. Several surgeons were involved, and we did the best we could to deal with the situation. My experiences as an intern or as a Navy doctor did little to prepare me for this type of tragedy.

One Saturday morning, I received a frantic call from the mother of a very healthy 13-year-old boy who had awakened with a high fever and a severe, unrelenting headache. We met at the emergency room. The boy looked gravely ill and was barely able to talk. Tests revealed he had bacterial meningitis and, despite IV antibiotics and corticosteroids, he lost consciousness. Many doctors and nurses were in attendance when my patient died a few hours later. He had experienced a full-system shutdown secondary to pneumococcal meningitis.

Medical school does not teach you how to talk to the family when such a devastating illness kills their 13-year-old, healthy child. Nor are we taught how to deliver other types of bad news, but it goes with the job description, and you must do it. It was probably the hardest part of being a doctor for me. There are no ground rules for things to say at such a time. When one is caring for a patient who dies, the needs of the family left behind can be enormous. Doctors try to help families cope with the grief and anger often present in these circumstances.

The first time my father came to visit, I was excited to have him witness his son, the doctor, at work in the profession we both loved.

He was finishing a bagel and coffee that first morning, and it was time for me to leave for work. I asked if he'd like to join me as I made my hospital rounds. His response was polite and poignant: *Does a mailman want to go for a walk when he's on vacation?*

But Dad was very pleased and proud that I had become a doctor. We would often discuss cases and frequently attended family practice meetings together. As father and son doctors, we attended fourteen Clinical Reviews for Family Doctors meetings at the Mayo Clinic in Rochester, Minnesota.

Many of the things I learned from Dad about being a doctor were not taught in medical school. *Treat all patients with respect* and *know when to refer* were two of his axioms I always followed. I cannot imagine a stronger father-son relationship than ours. Our political views may have differed, but we both believed that all people should have access to affordable, quality health care.

Many encounters with patients are memorable. A phone call from Mrs. Rogers to my office one day taught me that medications we prescribe can sometimes affect others. Mrs. Rogers was menopausal back in the days when monthly estrogen shots were the best way to combat the scourges of "that time" in the life of a woman when she must face daily hot flashes, irritability, mood swings, and unpredictable periods. Naturally, women so afflicted are frequently at odds with their spouses and children with whom they must interact daily. Mrs. Rogers was calling to schedule her monthly shot, and my receptionist dutifully asked, "What kind of shot is it that you need to get, Mrs. Rogers?" Her response to that question told the whole story: "Well, miss, I don't know the exact name of the shot but after I get it, within hours everyone around me starts acting nice again."

I did enjoy obstetrics. The goals of a healthy mom and full-term healthy baby were usually achievable. It was always exciting to deliver twins. One year, I delivered the baby of a 19-year-old woman and, a few months later, I delivered a baby for her 44-year-old mother. The grandchild was older than the teenage mother's sibling! However, in about 10% of obstetric cases, something will go awry. I remember delivering an 18-year-old woman's baby after a very protracted labor. Her uterus tore and the hemorrhaging was uncontrollable even with help from surgeons. She developed shock leading to kidney shutdown and had to be transferred to the University of Colorado Hospital in Denver. A hysterectomy was required to stop the bleeding. Happily, both mother and infant did well.

Early in my Longmont practice a patient and third-grade teacher named Annie asked if I would come to her class one day and "show and tell" something that might interest her students. That's an unusual challenge, I thought. I'm sure they don't want to hear a lecture on *anything* at age 9-11, but maybe if I brought some anatomical specimens preserved in formaldehyde I could elicit some wide eyes and get some curious questions. When I entered the classroom, the kids were abuzz with excitement and chatter. A hush came over the room as Miss Annie put her finger to her lips signaling the need to settle down. The brief silence was immediately broken when from my shopping bag I removed three jars, two with hearts and the other with a brain. The response exceeded what either the teacher or I had expected. There was a barrage of questions I knew would arise, but these attentive kids even seemed to understand my answers. I was stimulated by participating in such an unusual teaching situation.

Ms. Annie insisted that the students write thank you letters to me for coming to their class. Anyone who has ever had children, talked with children, or taught children knows this truth: Kids say the darndest things. There was a TV show on CBS from 1945 to 1967 called *Art Linkletter's House Party* that featured interviews of small children. That segment was named Kids Say the Darndest Things and often provoked the viewer to laugh out loud at the words that came out of the mouths of these cute kids—even before the acronym LOL was invented.

I have kept these handwritten letters written more than forty years ago. The following are some of them—without spell check— from my May 1974 guest appearance in that third-grade classroom.

1. Dear Dr. Wolf— Thank you giving us your time to for that great introduction of the heart and the brain. I especcily liked the brain. It looked so much like it was working. Sincerely, David

2. Dear Dr. Wolf— Thank you for showing us both hearts and the brain. Both hearts and brain were very interesting. My best thing of the whole thing was the heart. The inside was neat, and the vales (valves) were amazing. Sincerely, John

3. Dear Dad (from my son Dave, age 10)— I'm glad you decided to come today. I would have feeled sorry if you could not have. I guess I liked the brain the most. Thank you for becoming a doctor. Your guy, Dave

4. Dear Dr. Wolf— I realy liked when you showed the brain to us. Thank you for giving one hour of your time when you probably should have been in your office with a pationt. The heart was interesting too. Sincerely, Rodger

5. Dear Dr. Wolf— Thank you for sharing that stuf with us I liked that brain and the heart the chambers and all that stuf it is real neet. When I grow up, I am going to be a Dr. Sincerely, Ronnie

6. Dear Dr. Wolf— I really enjoyed your speech. I learned lots of things from it. I liked the hearts, but I liked the brain most. It was really exciting. Thank you for coming. I hope you liked our class. Sincerely, Frank

7. Dear Dr. Wolf— I like the brain because its inresting and good to your body. I enjoyed you coming today and I liked the heart because it helps you breath. My grampa had a heartatack and my mom and dad went to Ohio 10 or 20 weeks ago and we stayed in Boulder 2 days. Sincerely, Larry

8. Dear Dr. Wolf— Thanks for coming to the school and sharing what you know. I liked the brain and the hearts. You must know a lots of things about medicine and operating on people. You took one hour just for us. And you are probley very busy. Dave probley told you to come to our school. Sincerely, Brent

9. Dear Dr. Wolf— Thank you for comeing to talk to us. If you come again, try to bring a eye. I think it will be good to see. Sincerely, Bruce

10. Dear Dr. Wolf— I liked you brining the hearts and brain. They weren't relly all that bad. I thought it would be groze, but it relly wasn't. I thought that was very interesting sens we are studying the human body. Sincerely, Susan

11. Dear Doctor Wolf— I enjoied your visit very much. I am glad that you came because I like seeing the brain and hearts. It was exciting just to hear you talk. There is a girl I know how has two attached together half way. Sincerely, Kristine

12. Dear Dr. Wolf— Thank you for coming to the school to talk to us about the Hearts and the Brain. I wish you would come again and talk to us. I wish you could show us some more things about the body. Like the stomach so we can see it. Sincerely, Scott

13. Dear Dr. Wolf— I liked when you told us about the valves in the heart. It was interesting. Thank you for answering my question about what causes someone to have an extra finger. Sincerely, Jacque

14. Dear Dr. Wolf— Thank you for coming to our school. I liked the brain the best. It was real neat. The hearts was nice to. I would not like any body to take out my heart or any thing out of me. Sincerely, Kim

15. Dear Dr. Wolf— Thank you for showing a brain and two hearts for our unit on the human body. It has been a boreing unit. So I thank you for making it happier for us. Sincerely, Cooper

16. Dear Dr. Wolf— I am glad that you came to show the heart and the brain. I did a report on the heart. I wanted to see a real one but I knew I wouldn't see one but since good ole you brought it. I wish that everybody would not go sicko and grouse and yuk and stuff like that. That's all I have to say for now. Sincerely, Shelly

17. Dear Dr. Wolf— Thanks for showing us the brain and other stuff. I thought the brain was the neetest. The brain was about to make me erp up. Sincerely, Mark

18. Dear Dr. Wolf— Thanks for showing us the two hearts and the one brain. Special thanks for taking one hour off of work just for us. You really put your heart into it and your brain to. Sincerely, Matt

19. Dear Dr. Wolf— Thanks for coming. I learned a lot. I think you are very nice. My Aunt had a miscarriage once. And I have had strep throat two times in a row but I'm better now. Sincerely, Julie

• • •

About seven years later my activism gene stirred again. My son Dave was a player for the Longmont High School football team and not surprisingly, I attended all of his games. On one chilly and frosty night, LHS was playing at Greeley. The field's lights, with their thousands of bulbs, shone brightly through the autumn mist as they do all over America for home teams' Friday-night high school football games. The teams battled to a tie at halftime, but LHS eventually won the contest in a close game. As the teams headed for the locker room, Dave motioned to me to check out his injured elbow there. Because the coach knew me and knew I was a doctor, I was permitted to enter this usually sacred room. As I was examining my son's elbow, amidst the other dirty, sweaty teammates, the lights in the locker room were suddenly dimmed and everyone was asked to kneel, pray, and thank Jesus for the victory over Greeley Central.

I wrote letters to the Superintendent and Principal of LHS stating that, while I respect all religions, I could not condone prayer at any public school function. Be the prayers Christian, Muslim, Jewish, or another religion, clearly this was a violation of our constitution. If any of the LHS players happened not to be Christian, certainly he would have felt out of place and intimidated. I received a polite apology from the school in response and was assured that the locker room prayers would no longer be tolerated.

In the early 1970s, I volunteered to work in a hospital in Trujillo, Honduras, a small town on the Atlantic coast. It was an unforgettable experience being exposed to so many patients with anemia, malnutrition, and parasite infestations. The natives were always appreciative of *norteamericano* doctors and nurses who donated time and skill helping with basic health needs.

I was determined to learn as much español as I could. One morning in a small *comedor* (restaurant), a Honduran family was eating breakfast at a table adjacent to mine. I spotted a cereal box with the big rooster on their table and thought I'd seize the learning opportunity. I knew the Spanish word for corn was *maiz* but did not know how to say "flakes." I spoke to a little boy about six years old at that table, pointed to the cereal box, and asked: *"¿Como se dice en español?"* His answer came quickly but surprised me: *CORN FLAKES!*

Each summer the Longmont Clinic partnered with the Colorado State Migrant Council to take care of the basic medical needs of the seasonal migrant field workers. I really enjoyed these Hispanic patients and again marveled at their culture and language. In the late 1960s, however, state funding for migrant health care ended. Several other Longmont doctors and I volunteered to hold evening migrant clinic hours once weekly in a donated vacant house on Kimbark Street in downtown Longmont. This program lasted for several years and provided many patients with care they would not have otherwise received. Of course, there were other volunteers such as nurses, lab techs, and receptionists who helped make the migrant clinic possible.

Lafayette Practice

*I*n my nearly 54 years of practice, hardly a day went by that I didn't use these three little words: *I don't know.* It might have been a child's rash I couldn't promptly identify or an adult with atypical abdominal pain. Efforts to sift through diagnostic clues from the history and physical exams and then form logical, evidence-based assessments and treatment plans are among the rewarding challenges of medical practice. Sir William Osler, a famous professor of medicine more than 100 years ago, said: *Medicine is a science of uncertainty and an art of probability.*

Although I enjoyed many aspects of group practice at the Longmont Clinic, I did not like the frequent meetings or the inefficiencies inherent in a large institution. After eleven years, I resigned and accepted an invitation to join a solo family doctor in Lafayette, Colorado. Dr. Leon Gordon was happy to have some relief in his busy practice as he was nearing retirement. I began my Lafayette practice in January 1974 and, like my father, found my niche in running my own office.

Leon's office building at 401 E. Cleveland St. had the appearance of the dated family homes that surrounded it. It was not widely known that a steady stream of doctors had practiced at this address since 1914. Dr. Gordon added a pre-fab addition to this house while I saw patients in his historic office. Once completed, I rented this space from him until I ultimately bought the building in the early 1990s.

A large percentage of my patients in Lafayette were Hispanic. In the early days an elderly woman *(vieja)* patient told me interesting tales of the local *curandera*. They are considered witch doctors by some, but many believe in their magical herbs and cures. As in Galveston, when someone needed hospitalization, visiting relatives would usually fill the hospital room.

I took a week-long course in medical Spanish in Phoenix several years ago. I often tried to converse with my Spanish-speaking patients, but I learned most of my primitive grasp of the language from a retired Boulder High School Spanish teacher. From Argentina originally, Olga Hoffman was a very bright and compassionate social activist. Her methods of teaching me to write and speak Spanish were stern. I teased her about being so brutal in marking up my writing attempts. She charged no fee for her weekly tutoring sessions at her Boulder home. She even served coffee and *bizcochos* (cookies).

My early days in solo practice were unnerving at times. Except for a kindly old general practitioner from Louisville, Dr. Cassidy, there were no other primary care docs in either Lafayette or Louisville except semi-retired Dr. Gordon and me. Patients ranged in age from newborns to 100. A large number of my adult patients were employed by Storage Technology Corporation and the Rocky Flats Plant. A number of my former Longmont patients followed me to Lafayette so we were often extremely busy. We had an old X-ray machine and did our best to practice some limited orthopedics. There was no nearby hospital or urgent care. One busy afternoon, a frantic woman ran into the waiting room and asked if I was available to help with a home delivery a block away. The mom's regular doctor could not be there in time. Armed with a sterile pack of instruments, some syringes, and medications, an assistant and I followed the woman to the house barely in time to help deliver the healthy baby. The instruments and medications were not needed. Luckily, I had remembered to bring some umbilical tape to tie the cord.

Again, like on the USS Bayfield, I had no colleague to turn to when I needed immediate help or consultation. But in time I grew more confident and always kept in mind the adage from my father: *To be a good family doctor, you must know when and to whom to refer a patient.*

I had admitting privileges at Boulder Community Hospital and limited privileges at Longmont United. I had been on the staff of Avista Adventist Hospital since its inception in 1990 until my practice was purchased in 2011 by BCH. Throughout the years, I have assisted at surgery on my patients at all three hospitals when the surgeon felt my presence might be appropriate.

Early in my Lafayette practice, I learned that a grave illness may not disturb a regular guy. Duane was a stubborn 75-year-old farmer with pneumonia who needed to be hospitalized. He had been having chills and high fevers for a few days before seeking medical attention, and his exam revealed signs of severe pneumonia including rapid, labored breathing and poor color. I told him that failure to be admitted to the hospital for this illness could be fatal. But he had hay to put up and too many chores to do. It would be a waste of time to be lying around in a hospital, he reasoned. With prodding from family members, he finally acquiesced to my advice. While making rounds at BCH a few hours later, Duane — now in his hospital bed receiving oxygen and IV fluids containing antibiotics — looked better. Duane appeared to have "turned the corner" since his fever had broken and his breathing was no longer labored. When I asked how he was doing, his only expressed concern was that for three days he had not had a bowel movement — Duane's apparent barometer of his state of wellness. By the next day, he continued to show clinical improvement. Desiring the praise all doctors seek — the thanks for having helped a sick person get well — I again asked Duane if he was feeling better. Without a word of appreciation for what many folks had done to save his life, he again said his big worry was still his inability to move his bowels, despite the Milk of Magnesia I had ordered the night before. Unshaken, I said, "Hey, Duane, I just heard on the radio driving over here that the Colorado Legislature passed a bill that says you don't have to have a daily bowel movement!" His astonished look, and subsequent smile, told me that perhaps he'd succeed one day in tossing out his barometer.

Another lesson I learned early in my solo practice is that "ego trips can be cancelled." Having practiced in Longmont for more than eleven years, I had accumulated a sizable number of patients who considered me "their doctor." When I moved thirty minutes away to my Lafayette solo practice, I was pleased to welcome former Longmont patients. I'll acknowledge that I was on a bit of an "ego trip." After all, I must be a pretty good doc for patients to follow me that far. That all changed when Mrs. Kelley, the stoic matriarch of a farm family whom I had attended when I practiced in Longmont, put it this way, "Well, Doc, the old man and I talked it over and decided we'd start comin' down here to see you...." I was ready to set sail on yet another ego trip, but then she added, "We decided it ain't that yer' such a good doctor or nuthin' like that, it's jes' too damn much hassle to change." My ego trips were cancelled until further notice!

Most of my practice years were in Lafayette. I was fortunate for more than 30 of those years to have a dependable, competent, and affable office manager, Ruth Farley. Many family doctors in the 1970s and 1980s resisted the influx of non-physician practitioners such as physician assistants and nurse practitioners. Dr. Gordon, who had helped set me up in practice in Lafayette, was adamant that "nobody but a doctor should be examining patients and prescribing for them." I did not share his views. In fact, every year of my practice, I employed PAs and/or NPs and was involved in several student preceptorship programs. Nurses are the hub of a busy family practice and I was fortunate to have had several excellent nurses on my staff. Besides providing proficient care to patients in our practice, my employees allowed me to enjoy days off and vacation time.

The cliché *"laughter is the best medicine"* has inspired me to record some memorable vignettes. Most patients' names have been changed, in case you thought I might be violating patient privacy rules!

A few years ago, John, a patient of mine in his 60s, underwent back surgery for scoliosis. This condition had caused pain and deformity for much of his life. The spine surgery involved the insertion of a metal rod in the spinal column to straighten the deformity and take pressure off the impinged nerve roots. As a result, such patients usually gain an inch or so of height. John and his wife, Sharon, came to see me several weeks after the successful operation. I commented that not only was his chronic pain mostly relieved and the deformity corrected, but he had gained a full inch and a half in height when his spine became straightened! I playfully asked Sharon, his soft-spoken wife of many years, how she felt living with a husband who had become taller. Her response nearly laid me out with laughter. "Well, Doc, I'm still waiting for 'dark and handsome.'"

One day an attractive young woman in her twenties presented to my office as a new patient with a respiratory infection. After I had examined her and as I was writing a prescription, she hesitantly said, "Dr. Wolf, I don't know if I you should tell you this or not...." I wondered if I had visible spinach between my front teeth, or worse, that my fly was open. "What is it?" I boldly asked. She replied: "When you were in Longmont you delivered me!" What a nice surprise for me!

Pediatricians and family docs caring for children often reward their little patients who exhibit good behavior during the patient encounter. Because of dental health issues, we quit offering candy or lollipops. Balloons were once popular, but the risk of suffocation or swallowing has discontinued that type of reward. So we resorted to stickers, those colorful little items kids love and mothers sometimes forget to remove on laundry day. Some feature cartoon characters, space kids, athletes, and cute animals. There are even those that seem destined to evoke arguments about gender such as "Boys Rule" and "Girls Rule."

Four-year-old Tommy was a trooper during his office visit for an ear infection. I showed him our vast array of stickers. His selection was thoughtful and quick. He passed over the cool Spider Man and dragon and other animal choices. Tommy pointed to the "Girls Rule" sticker. That was the one he wanted. I pointed to the "Boys Rule" emblem, but he did not budge. He wanted the one that announced that Girls Rule! I looked to the little boy's mother and asked, "How can Tommy know at age four know what it took me nearly 40 years to figure out?"

During my years in Lafayette, I volunteered in health-related fields to "give back" to the community and county in which I worked. I served as a director on the Boulder County Board of Health for ten years and as president two of those years. I also volunteered in the Health Department's STD clinic. I received a Victim's Assistance Award from the County and was awarded VFW of Lafayette Citizen of the Year in 1992. I helped start the Boulder County Medical

Society's Physician's Care Program, where patients lacking insurance could see specialist physicians enrolled in the program for a mere $10.

As I was nearing my 40th year in my Lafayette solo practice, it was clear that this quaint little office practice could not be sustained financially. Insurance payments dwindled and expenses increased. Several times I had to raid my savings account to meet payroll. Nationwide, small practices such as mine were being acquired by nearby hospitals. In 2011 I sold my practice to Boulder Community Hospital. They paid me rent and I worked in my same office for two years adapting fairly well as an employed corporate physician. I was grateful for the opportunity to continue to practice. But I turned down their offer to continue beyond my two-year contract.

TEACHING

I found myself enjoying teaching experiences, whether it was doing show-and-tell to 3rd graders in Longmont or serious teaching and preceptoring of medical, physician assistant, or nurse practitioner students in my Lafayette office. Our office served as an excellent clinical setting for learning how to take care of patients. We cared for patients of all ages, sizes, and colors for many different conditions. It was stimulating to watch these future practitioners—now called health care providers—learn the skills of history taking, physical exam, assessment, and treatment plans. What matters most, I would preach, is to treat all patients with dignity and respect. A famous professor of medicine, Sir William Osler, again: *The good physician treats the disease. The great physician treats the patient with the disease.*

I can recall more than one student who appeared to speak down to patients. I always tried to teach humility because I believe practitioners and patients should have equal interest in achieving positive results from the encounters. We providers do not "know it all" and when we come across as too arrogant, the relationship between practitioner and patient is compromised. The limits of our knowledge should be part of who we are as clinicians.

A much lighter example of teaching includes the many years I volunteered to be involved in the local school district's "Sex Ed" presentations for 5th and 6th graders. The classroom would be filled with many nervous, giggling girls and raucous boys awaiting information on the perils of puberty. First there was a narrated, low budget slide show produced by the Colorado Department of Health that addressed the main issues. For the lively Q and A that followed I was often accompanied by Betsy Barringer, a terrific PA from my office staff. After one of these slide shows at Erie Public School, it was time for their written questions to be answered. Of course, in such an outrageous and highly charged situation where both pubertal boys and girls can do the asking, it was important to have anonymity. Each student shielded the torn-off piece of notebook paper on which they scribbled their personal concerns and questions. Betsy and I learned the true meaning of the word *aplomb* when forcing ourselves not to laugh while reading these treasures aloud to the class and trying to provide meaningful, helpful answers. Again, spell check turned off:

1. When a man and woman have sex and girl does not have the egg where it should be, what happens?
2. What happens when you are fully mature and have your period but that was three months ago?
3. What kind of "sex chewall" feeling do men get?
4. Why do boys have "wet dreams?"
5. How does a baby come out of a girl?
6. When do you get hair on your chest?
7. At what age do sex hormones stop working?
8. Does a girl know exactly when her period starts or will it just come and you don't know it?
9. How long is puberty? What about adelesince?
10. Why do you grow hair down there? What is the purpose?
11. What happens if the baby doesn't come out?
12. If my Mom started her period when she was 11, when will I start mine?
13. How long is the average sized penis?

14. Does a boy have anything like a period?
15. How does the baby get out of the vagina?
16. What happens if one of the testacels gets smashed?
17. Is it fun or a good experience to make love or have intercourse?
18. How do you tell your parents about periods?
19. Is there any kind of pills you can take when you have cramps? I'm going right now and jest wanted to say it's not going to be too bad.
20. Do the eggs have to be fertilized during your period?
21. Why do boys pop bonners?
22. How do you tell your mom you had your period?
23. Can you swim while your on your period?
24. Why do you have to menstruate?
25. How do the sparm cell get into the woman?
26. Do you skip a period when you are pregnant or right before?
27. Where do you throw youre tampon out in school? Cause it might make an odor in the trash.
28. What do you do if your taking a bath or shower and your period starts?
29. What happens if you have a baby and then the next month another egg gets fertilized?
30. What makes you feel different about boys as you get older?
31. Can a woman have a baby without having sex?
32. When a woman gets older she doesn't have a period. Does the same sort of thing happen to a man?
33. How does a girl act when she gets turned on?
34. What is a ogoasem?
35. Should you have sex before or after a girls period?
36. Where does the sperm go if there is no egg in the uterus?
37. If two sperms reach the egg what happens?
38. When a women is pregnit what happens if they have sex?
39. Boys peneiss gets stiff. What happens to girls?

40. How come some girls have big breast and some little?

41. Why do people have a nessesery feeling for sex?

42. I know this girl that when she goes to the bathroom she has white gluppy stuff on her underwear. What is this?

43. If you have your period and your suppose to take a shower wouldn't the blood go everywhere?

44. What color will your child be if you have sexual intercourse with a colored person?

45. What happens when a baby comes out the wrong way?

46. How big can your testicals get?

47. Does it hurt to master bate?

48. What if blood goes through your pants at school and people call you names?

49. How many times do you have to have sex to get pregnant?

50. Does sex make you tired?

51. Do you get in grumpy moods when your haaving your period?

52. How come grownups talk about sex so much?

Clinica Campesina

*I*n the spring of 1977, a group of Lafayette citizens led by Alicia Sanchez , her daughter, Eleanor Montour, Pete Garcia, and Cecilia Garcia (no relation) began to forge the beginnings of Clinica Campesina Family Health Services, a place where the uninsured and underinsured could access basic health care. Prior to Clinica's beginning, Alicia, Eleanor, and others had often taken financially strapped patients needing care to the University of Colorado Hospital in Denver. This group asked for my support of Clinica and they received it.

As an activist for health care reform, I am sadly aware that the uninsured and other low-income people are not able financially to access care. To start Clinica required leadership, courage, and money. Besides requiring a highly functioning medical clinic to serve thousands of people, there were other needs. Finding the right personnel, an energetic CEO, a core of administrative staff, a strong board of directors, and an army of volunteers were ongoing needs for the nearly 40 years of Clinica's existence. In my view, they have met these requirements.

Front row: Pauline Romano (CEO), Joanna Savarese, R.N., Inez Buggs, N.P.,
Eleanor and Tony Montour, and Howie.
Back row: Phyllis Greene (board member) and Wilford Buggs.

I helped train Inez Buggs in her quest to become a nurse practitioner, and she subsequently worked at Clinica in that capacity for 30 years! A Boulder family practitioner, the late Dr. Bill Salter, and I served as Clinica's first medical directors, but Inez saw the bulk of the patients during her thirty years of work there. At a retirement dinner honoring Inez's compassionate care, her skills, and her dedication, each table had a box of tear-catching tissues to be used as needed by staff, friends, and family. Alicia, too, was honored as a pillar of the community by having an elementary school in Lafayette named for her: *ALICIA SANCHEZ ELEMENTARY.*

Several months after her retirement, I asked Inez if she would like to work part time in my office and she said "yes." Even in her 70s, Nurse Practitioner Inez Buggs continued to be proficient and compassionate in her care of patients.

Under the determined and brilliant leadership of CEO Pete Leibig, tens of thousands of patients annually receive exemplary medical care for little or no cost. Most of the patients seen would be unable to access care without community health clinics such as Clinica. This institution has become a national model for delivering needed services to patients. A story about Clinica's diabetes management approach was featured on Jim Lehrer's *PBS NewsHour*. As a community health center, Clinica receives much of its income from governmental sources and foundations, but private donations are their lifeblood.

Pete was at the helm when Clinica opened health centers in Adams County, Thornton, and in 2009 he helped to facilitate a major merger with the Boulder's well-known People's Clinic. Hundreds of thousands of patients who lack insurance or who are on Medicaid are served annually by these community clinics. Clinica is now building a new facility in Lafayette.

Activities

$\mathcal{S}$ince I began my practice in Colorado, I have been active in medical society and family practice organizations. I have been a member, a delegate, and a board member of the Boulder County Medical Society and the Colorado Medical Society. I have served on many committees within both organizations. In 1972, I served as president of the Colorado Academy of Family Physicians. I also served as a CAFP board member and delegate to the American Academy of Family Physicians. I have served on the boards of the Boulder County Public Health, the Community Medical Center in Lafayette, and was a regular member for nearly fourteen years on the Eastern Boulder County Child Protection team. In this latter group, I was astounded to learn of the frequency and nature of child abuse in our society.

In April 2010, my wife, Rose Pierro, and I volunteered with a group of about 25 others for a medical mission to Peru. The mission was sponsored by the Global Health Initiative Project of Centura Health. We flew to Lima and then to Iquitos, which is near the headwaters of the Amazon River. Each day of the mission, we went on a river boat to different villages examining and treating hundreds of patients who lived along this amazing river. Like in Honduras, the natives were most appreciative for the care they received. Part of our group included three ophthalmologists who performed

Howie and wife, Rose Pierro.

cataract surgery at an Iquitos hospital and in four days restored the sight of more than seventy blind Peruvians!

Most of the villagers I saw were friendly, smiling, and happy that some *norteamericanos* were there to help them. However, one woman of 83 had a frown on her face when she presented to me for care. I asked, *"Que es la problema, senora?"* She exclaimed, *"Oh, doctor, tengo arthritis en mi rodilla!* (I have arthritis in my knee!)" I responded: *"Yo, tambien!"* (So do I!). She not only smiled but laughed heartily. She saw humor in the fact the doctor who was assigned to treat her knee pain had exactly the same problem as did she!

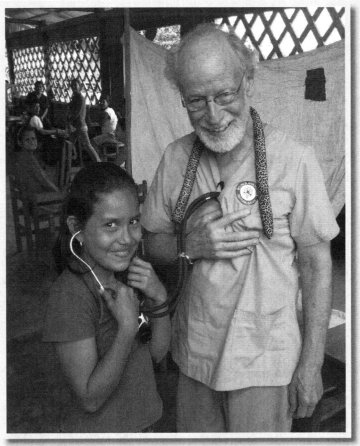

The would-be doctor native girl who wouldn't stop flirting with the norteamericano.

In July 2013 Rose and I again volunteered for a medical mission with Global Health Initiatives, backed by Centura Health. This time our mission was in Rwanda, but instead of eye specialists we brought two volunteer orthopedic surgeons, an anesthesiologist plus three OR nurses. This

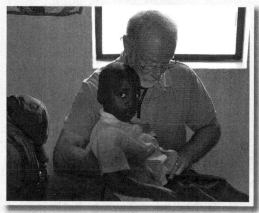

Physical exam of five-year-old Rwandan boy.

African journey consisted of breath-taking beauty, mind-boggling history, and an obvious awareness of the lack of basic needs of many people. It had been nearly twenty years since the senseless 1994 genocide, not a civil war as it was initially labeled by the UN. Unspeakable photos of the slaughter were displayed at the Genocide Museum in Kilgali, the capital of Rwanda. We traveled by bus to the western region of the country known as the "land of a thousand hills" to provide care at the Mugonero Adventist Hospital and nearby orphanage. The first two hours of the three-hour journey featured an asphalt road with very sharp curves on mountainsides which regularly displayed gorgeous scenery and many tiny villages. Every few kilometers were Rwandans, mostly women, walking while carrying various products and containers on their heads. The last hour of travel on that hot and muggy day was not for those of us burdened with motion sickness. The narrow dirt road which ascended to the hospital had even more curves per mile and offered no lengthy straight stretches.

The Adventist Mugonero hospital is quite old and located in a rural area far from any village of size. It consisted of several brick buildings, mostly in good condition. Each day the surgeons, anesthesiologist, and nurses operated on several patients, mostly those with fractures weeks to months old and often associated with infected skin wounds. I made rounds with doctors on the internal medicine, pediatric, and OB wards. In my 50+ years of family medicine, I had seen but one case of malaria, already diagnosed and treated by the VA. But in this hospital each day five to seven patients were receiving IV medications for this disease. I saw two patients with liver abscesses from parasites and several cases of TB.

Rose stayed at the nearby orphanage and provided help in many ways. I did physicals on kindergarten children there one morning. Most were somewhat anemic and malnourished, but very lively and well-behaved.

Reflecting on such global volunteer efforts, one wonders if spending a week or so is actually beneficial to the people, whether in Peru or Rwanda. But a frequent volunteer named Kim Coats said it best: "Don't think that what you do here has no lasting effect, because we offer these people hope that someone cares about them and wants to see them succeed."

Road between hospital and orphanage.

Examining an Old Adage: Doctors Should Avoid Lawyers

*A*fter becoming a doctor, my dad unceremoniously proclaimed to me an old adage: *Never ever testify against another doctor in a malpractice case.* Doctors do the best they can, he said, but we are not perfect. Greedy lawyers will capitalize on those mistakes, but they need doctors to testify as expert witnesses against the accused doctors. You must never do that. It's just an unwritten rule.

Early in my practice, I had a patient who was a bright young lawyer, Bill Taylor—not his real name. I was taken by surprise one day when he asked if I would take a look at a malpractice case. "No," I responded quickly with determination considering the strong imprint of the adage delivered by my dad. A few weeks later, he again pleaded unsuccessfully. Then, about a month later Bill said: "Howie, I just want you to take look at this case and tell me if you think what this physician did falls below the standard of care for a family doctor." I cautiously relented. This was a case where a woman patient with recurrent abdominal pain would meet her family doctor at his office at night and he'd give her a shot of a narcotic to relieve her pain. Then he would have sex with her. The accused doctor admitted in his deposition that this was true. The woman ended up divorced and in drug rehab.

Despite the admonition from Dad, I felt compelled to do the right thing and testify, in a court of law if necessary, that what this doctor did was egregious. I accepted the challenge and realized what I must do. I knew there would be a malpractice insurance company lawyer or two defending the doctor, quizzing me about my qualifications, my thorough knowledge of the case, especially about the narcotic given, and why I would be willing to testify against one of my brethren medical colleagues.

This took place many years before the internet. I knew I must learn all I could about the pharmacology of the narcotic given — its chemical properties, its side effects, and its addictive potential. This meant that during times when I was not seeing patients, usually on a day off, I would drive to Denver to access the University of Colorado Medical School Library. I made several trips there taking many notes readying myself for the defending attorney's cross-examinations.

Adorned in suit and tie as an "expert" should be, I went through depositions from both plaintiff and defendant attorneys. Present at all such testimony is a recorder whose extraordinary stenographic skills become entries for official documents. The dark paneled meeting room at the defendant attorney's office reeked of furniture polish and set a gloomy tone. I was somewhat nervous when I began responding to the barrage of questions, but I remained confident that I was on the right side of this case. I was examined, cross-examined, and my deposition was thus recorded. The date of the trial was set.

Many thoughts whizzed through my head. Was I doing the right thing? Should I even tell my dad about my transgression? I held no one in higher esteem than my dad. Would he feel ashamed of what I had done or would he be pleased at my decision to testify against a doctor whose actions were so despicable? How would I feel about facing a jury and discussing my opinions? Would I be able to look the defendant doctor in the eye as I testified? Would I look, feel, and be "the expert?"

On the day of the trial, the case was mercifully settled. I felt relieved but also some pride that I had done the right thing.

I assumed this would be the only time I'd be asked to look at a potential malpractice case. I was wrong. A couple of years later a lawyer from Boulder called me. He was representing a plaintiff who had been mistreated at a doctor's office and was considering a malpractice suit, thus seeking censure and compensation. He asked me to review the voluminous paperwork involved. Having shed the "old adage" onus, I took on this challenge, too. My conclusion: This was not malpractice. The records revealed that defendant doctor and his receptionist had horrific manners and treated the plaintiff patient in a rude, dismissive fashion. No injury or delay in treatment occurred so instead of a malpractice suit without merit, I suggested a letter be written to the county and state medical societies, where grievance committees review such complaints and elicit responses from the accused physician. I knew this was the proper venue to have the complaints reviewed because I had served several years on the Boulder County Medical Society Grievance Committee. This case typifies the kinds of cases that are reviewed and, when indicated, reprimands and suggestions are given. Sadly, many health professionals do not treat patients with dignity and respect.

From author Malcolm Gladwell in his book *Blink*: "The overwhelming number of people who suffer an injury due to the negligence of a doctor never file a malpractice claim at all. Patients don't file lawsuits because they've been harmed by shoddy medical care. Patients file lawsuits because they've been harmed by shoddy medical care and...patients say they were rushed or ignored or treated poorly."

While I was in my Lafayette solo practice, I had the freedom to become involved in reviewing and testifying in medical malpractice cases. I could pick and choose. There must be an underground network of malpractice lawyers who can identify and secure expert witnesses in all medical specialties. I was getting regular calls from lawyers who had heard that I had a respectable reputation as a family practice expert witness. Over a period of forty years, I probably reviewed more than fifty cases. I gave depositions in at least half of those and appeared in court about ten times.

A 28-year-old woman underwent a bilateral mastectomy because a family practice clinic failed to adequately follow up an imaging study that showed a small mass in one breast. The X-ray appearance of the lesion was that it was solid, rather than cystic, and could be a harbinger of breast cancer. During the next year and a half, the patient was seen in the clinic by other providers for other reasons, but no one reminded her she had a potentially serious problem. This 18-month delay in diagnosis and treatment was clearly responsible for her poor outcome. For me to adequately prepare for the imminent interrogation at deposition time, I needed to bone up on relevant medical data. At the deposition, I was asked to back up my opinion that the delay in treatment was a significant factor. To their dismay, the information I quoted from reputable medical journals was irrefutable. This case was settled in favor of the plaintiff.

I was asked by COPIC, a Colorado malpractice insurance company, to consider defending a case where their insured defendant doctor was being sued for negligence in his treatment of a man who had sustained a leg injury. When I inspect relevant information in such a case, I'm scrutinizing the doctor's records, hospital records, as well as depositions by the plaintiffs, other witnesses, and the defendant. I would have been delighted to testify in defense of a fellow physician, but, after reviewing the records, I concluded that the injuries sustained by the plaintiff were not treated in an appropriate or timely manner. My response to the insurance company was that I felt the case was indefensible. Hopefully my opinion meant the case woud be settled, thus avoiding a costly trial.

All doctors make mistakes. Those who say they never have done so are, in my view, simply liars! It's when the mistakes cause significant life-changing injuries or death that the physician's medical malpractice company and its army of defense lawyers should become involved. This is precisely why almost all practicing physicians carry such insurance. Cases that are indefensible should be settled. Cases where the evidence of an accused doctor's records indicate no breach of standard of care must be vigorously defended.

A Wyoming lawyer I'll call Frank Collier contacted me to review a case in which he was defending a family doctor. A year earlier I had enjoyed working with Mr. Collier on the side of a plaintiff in another delayed diagnosis case. Of course, I would be delighted to find a situation where I could stand on the side of a brother or sister family doctor colleague. This latest case involved a man in his sixties who was seen by the defendant doctor when she (I'll call her Dr. Ellen) was on call for a small Wyoming town's hospital emergency room. The patient's history was important because he had undergone heart by-pass surgery two months earlier in Utah. Things were going well, but on a chilly Wyoming week-end he developed flu-like symptoms with fever, chills, muscle aches, and vomiting. He went to the local hospital's ER.

Dr. Ellen was on call and her notes were impeccable as she described her exam, her diagnosis, and her plan of treatment. She admitted the man to the hospital because of his viral illness and dehydration; she then properly administered IV fluids. When making rounds the next morning, she found the patient much improved and anxious to go home. He did complain of slight pain in his left calf and Dr. Ellen naturally had a concern about a DVT, a deep vein thrombosis or blood clot. Her thorough exam was negative for edema (swelling) or demonstrable tenderness. It was Sunday, and to get the proper imaging study would involve getting the on-call technician to come to the hospital. The patient declined the imaging study and insisted on going home. Later that night, the patient developed a blood clot in his lung and died.

The deceased's family sued Dr. Ellen for failing to order a scan, which would likely have shown a blood clot. Anticoagulants could then have been started and the patient's clot might not have traveled to his lung and he likely would have survived. There were many documents to review: the hospital records, the records of the patient's by-pass surgery, and the depositions of all parties.

Lawyer Collier's assistant made the arrangements and sent a round-trip ticket for me to fly from Colorado to Wyoming for the trial. I was certain a mistake had been made when I saw the ticket showing that the carrier was Great Lakes Airlines. Everyone knows there are no Great Lakes anywhere near Wyoming! But, indeed, on a brisk fall afternoon I flew from Denver's DIA airport to Rock Springs, Wyoming, aboard a 19-passenger GLA plane. I was met by Frank Collier, his assistant, and Dr. Ellen. We went from the airport to dinner at a typical Wild West tavern/restaurant to discuss strategy in the defense of Dr. Ellen. I knew we were in Wyoming when I spotted a guy at the restaurant wearing an "I Hate Tree Huggers" t-shirt.

Dr. Ellen was just starting her career. She had trained in the Midwest and completed a family practice residency. She was smart, and it was clear that she was a caring doctor and distraught at the notion of facing a malpractice suit early in her career. Nothing in the records showed a deviation from the standard of care, but I was certain the plaintiff's lawyers would pounce on anything to incriminate the young doctor. In my opinion, even though the patient succumbed, Dr. Ellen should not be faulted.

The small-town Wyoming courtroom was filled with people, mostly friends and family of the deceased. I offered testimony to the lawyers representing both sides. There were many questions on direct and cross-examination. How could it be, the plaintiff's lawyer asked, that this relatively young man, who was recovering nicely from his heart by-pass surgery, winds up dead after a simple viral illness? Isn't it true that lying in that hospital bed overnight provided him many hours of immobility and that such prolonged lack of movement could predispose him to a blood clot? Shouldn't Dr. Ellen have been aware of this information and ordered the scan just to rule out a DVT—even though it was a Sunday? Isn't it true that had a scan been done, the clot would've been found and anticoagulation begun? We wouldn't be in this courtroom today had the patient survived, would we, Dr. Wolf?

Although the questions were accusatory, some good points were raised. Yet, Dr. Ellen had done everything a reasonable family doctor should have done. Had her exam of the leg revealed swelling or had the physical exam testing for DVT been positive, I told the lawyer and the jury I believed Dr. Ellen would have ordered the scan. She did all the right things and her patient died anyway. All physicians or other providers who care for the ill have experienced this phenomenon.

Not satisfied, the plaintiff's lawyer came back at me with more on the immobility issue. Isn't it true, Dr. Wolf, that even long airplane flights can predispose one to DVT's and that's why passengers are encouraged to get up and walk about? Many flights, he continued, are about the same length of time that the deceased lay in bed at the hospital. I pondered the connection he was trying to make and then responded carefully. Are you suggesting, counselor, that all airlines be required to provide a scan for all passengers who have been on long flights? The absurdity of this notion caused several of the jurors and many in the courtroom to laugh.

Happily, Dr. Ellen was exonerated. Our legal defense team felt that my testimony, especially the coup de grace about airlines, had been crucial in our defense. Having helped the young doctor escape the perils of a medical malpractice suit made me feel like our team had just won the Super Bowl!

George Penfield — not his real name — was a lawyer from a large Colorado city. He asked if I would consider being an expert witness in a case involving a nine-year-old boy named Juan. George said he rarely did medical malpractice cases, but Juan was his own son's friend and playmate. For more than a year, the boy's parents had taken Juan to a large family practice clinic with symptoms of vomiting and weight loss. He was seen on different dates by several different clinic physicians. Juan's symptoms were attributed to the stress of his older sister moving away from home to get married. He was even hospitalized in a mental hospital for a few weeks but this was not beneficial and the boy continued to vomit and lose weight. Several different medications were tried without benefit. Finally, one of the clinic doctors suggested Juan might have a brain tumor and suggested an imaging study be done but failed to order the test. Several months and several doctor visits later, a scan was finally ordered, and it showed a brain tumor located in the front of his brain pressing on the optic nerve. Juan was then referred to Children's Hospital in Denver, where the tumor was carefully removed, but he suffered permanent visual and cognitive impairments.

Mr. Penfield and I met before the deposition. I did have a certain amount of angst about facing the clinic's lawyer, but was confident in my opinion that Juan had suffered permanent visual and mental damage, likely due to the long delay in diagnosis and treatment of his brain tumor.

Imagine my surprise when I walked into the dark and dingy deposition room and realized that each of the seven clinic doctors who had examined Juan had her or his own lawyer! I felt like the biblical Daniel in the den of lions! Each lawyer carefully parceled out the part of the record involving the doctor he or she represented. Then I was quizzed in this fashion by each one: Well, Dr. Wolf, please look at my client's note on this date. Do you see evidence of malpractice of failure to adhere to the standard of care by my client here on this date? When the record and doctor visits were separated in this way, it was impossible to pin down just who was at fault. But when looked at completely, it was clear that the clinic's care for Juan was deficient in addressing his worrisome symptoms in a timely manner. Nine-year-old kids gain weight, I said, they do not lose weight if they are healthy. In my view, the doctors who were involved in Juan's care were collectively at fault for the poor outcome. The case was settled and the family was awarded an undisclosed sum of money.

I was asked by a Miami attorney to look at a case where a doctor there saw a fifty-year-old man with pressure-like pain in his neck, chest, and abdomen. Without doing any tests, the doctor gave the patient a medication for heartburn. The patient died that evening of a massive heart attack. To me this was failure to diagnose a serious and potentially fatal condition. Any adult with pain such as described by this man deserves to have diagnostic studies — including an EKG and lab work — to rule out a heart problem. The attorney had me fly first-class to Miami and I was put up in a snazzy hotel. I had never flown first-class before and I certainly lapped it up! I spread out the paperwork from the Miami case on my tray table. took notes, drank some champagne, and consumed a tasty dinner. What a treat!

I gave my deposition the next day and then flew back to Denver. I learned later from the Florida lawyer that the case was settled, and the doctor was found guilty of malpractice.

So how about that adage about testifying against a fellow doctor? In my view, having an understanding about "standard of care" for a family physician expert witness is crucial. While the term is rather vague, it does convey a concept that competent family doctors understand. The obvious example was the case of the doctor meeting his female patient in the office to provide drugs and sex. Most cases are not so obvious. All of us—health care providers, caregivers, and patients—must accept certain facts. Just because someone dies, one cannot conclude that the provider was at fault, or his handling of the case fell below the standard of care. Just because a baby is born and has brain damage does not mean the obstetrician or midwife messed up somehow.

Throughout my career, I've met many competent lawyers, some more affable than others. These interactions taught me how the law applies in each case and I can then offer how a reasonable and prudent family doctor might handle it. Therefore, doctor and lawyer alike have information which determines how to proceed. Hopefully I saved the system money when, after reviewing a potential malpractice suit, I state to the lawyer my opinion that the plaintiff does not have a winnable case.

Several times I was asked to be a medical expert by Scott McComas, a young, proficient, and conscientious Boulder lawyer. Scott was often the designated-by-the-court lawyer to represent down-and-out clients with the most bizarre legal battles.

In one case, Scott was defending a man who was a known alcoholic who had driven his car across the median and struck an oncoming car. No one was injured seriously, but an elderly woman in the back seat of the other car sustained a hip fracture. After the hip pinning surgery, the woman developed a minor urinary tract infection, which was treated and improved. Nearly two years later, she died in a nursing home from an illness that began as a urinary infection. The family sued, alleging the accident indirectly caused her death. Scott conceded that his client was drunk and had broken the law by crossing the median. But he asked me if this woman's death might have been related in any way to the accident so long ago. My conclusion was that it was not.

There was the well-publicized case of the driverless car in Boulder county. No, this was not of the robotic type. In this case eight young people amply plied with beer at a Longmont tavern took a ride in a borrowed Chevy Blazer with a detachable roof. They were speeding on a country dirt road which ran parallel to a large irrigation ditch lined with a row of trees. The careless driver swerved and the vehicle plunged into the ditch. The detachable roof became detached as the Blazer struck a tree branch causing most of the passengers to be thrown from the car. One young man was killed. Scott was defending the driver, Tim, who became the "alleged driver," because Tim insisted that Maggie, one of the women in the car, was the actual driver. Of course, Maggie denied the accusation and my expert witness sleuth activities included looking at several photographs of Maggie's injuries and dozens of photographs of the completely totaled car. To me, the evidence was inconclusive and there was at least a possibility, based on the evidence I had pored over, that Maggie could have been the driver. At the trial, the DA even proclaimed: This was a stupid car accident where the car was full of drunks. A man was killed. Damn it, someone had to have been driving the frigin' car! Eventually, Tim took the rap in the driverless car saga.

Final Chapter

UPDATE OF
"I REALLY DIDN'T WANT TO BECOME A DOCTOR"
JULY 2016

*M*y initial book, *I Really Didn't Want to Become a Doctor*, ended with me working for two years in my Lafayette office as an employed physician of Boulder Community Hospital. I was offered a contract to continue working for BCH after my contract ended on March 31, 2013.

I had visions of restarting my solo practice, but it was not financially feasible. I was reminded of two old aphorisms: If you've tried something once and it didn't work, it's unlikely you'll get a different result if you try again. And, in the advice given by George Bernard Shaw to a friend about to re-marry his ex-wife that such an attempt would represent the triumph of hope over reality.

An article about me appeared that April in *the Boulder Daily Camera* indicating that I had ended my Lafayette practice of nearly forty years. A family practitioner from nearby Broomfield, Dr. Elisabeth Kandel, spotted the piece and called me to see if I'd be interested in working part time in a Thornton office. She and her husband, also a family doc, Dr. David Leistikow, had been acquaintances of mine from many years earlier through the Colorado Academy of Family Physicians. They own Family Medicine Associates of Broomfield and Thornton, and it happened that the family doctor who preceded me in FMA's Thornton office would be retiring in September 2013.

The offer caused me to ponder what might lie ahead. I was a mere 78 years old then, and still felt the desire to continue seeing patients, helping in any way I could. My father practiced until he was 88, and I remember questioning him when he was in his early 80s as to why he wanted to continue to work. "It's what I do best, and the work gives me pleasure," was his candid response.

Henry Wolf and Howie Wolf discussing an array of important topics.

We had often conversed through the years, comparing and contrasting our styles of practice and our attitudes toward the rapidly changing events which had influenced medical practice. He was still making house calls for patients who had difficulty coming to his office. He had given up doing obstetrics at age 79, whereas I had quit when I was about 35, when the first obstetrician joined the Longmont Clinic. Dad's mind remained sharp and his skillful calming and reassuring manner had helped many patients and their families through countless crises.

But he did lose some of his zest for medicine, exemplified by his resentment of government and insurance company intrusions. Dad dispensed medicine from his office and "Those damn bureaucrats came in one day on a judge's order and caused havoc." They went through the bottles and packages of pills he was dispensing and left without cleaning up the mess they left behind. Nor was Dad accustomed to the required paperwork documentation for his hospitalized patients, so he didn't do it. He steadfastly refused to sign Medicare forms, and did not take their phone calls or answer their letters.

However, if you were a patient of Doc Wolf's and had Medicare, you could see a doctor in a neighboring town for a $21 office call, submit a claim to Medicare and receive $11 back about two or three months later. Or you could see Doc Wolf for $10 and avoid the delay and paperwork! Further, if you had trouble paying for needed care, he would see you for little or no charge. Should you be too proud to accept such charity, the old barter system remained operational.

Dad kept up with changes in clinical medicine by reading journals and attending meetings. His favorite meetings were the Mayo Clinic's annual Family Practice Clinical Reviews which he had attended most years since they began in 1948. He and I attended as father and son for 14 of those years. He was a charter member of the American Academy of General Practice, now known as the American Academy of Family Physicians. I was a member of AAFP during all my years of practice.

No son could have loved, appreciated, or respected his father more than I did, but the generation gap did spell some interesting differences, too. Though I resented bureaucratic tangles as much as my father and had written my share of poison pen letters to insurance companies, including Medicare's contractor, my office always tried to cope and comply with the multiplicity of problems inherent in these systems. And I participated in at least two activities my father always considered quasi-unethical: peer review and working with lawyers. In neither did I consider myself superior to other FP's, but felt I was qualified as other family docs to do chart review on peers, an activity that was required by hospitals. My association with lawyers consisted of consulting on potential or active malpractice cases, as discussed in the "Examining an Old Adage" chapter. I did document my care of patients both in and out of the hospital setting. But my father and I would have both agreed that the measure of a good doctor is not the quantity or quality of records, but the overall regard and respect for the patient as a human being—regardless of race, religion, sexual orientation or financial status. I continued to follow in the footsteps of the man I held in such high esteem.

I decided to accept the job offer from Family Medicine Associates and worked three mornings per week from September 2013 to July 2016. The main challenges were that most of our patients were on pain management and most were on Medicaid. I did have several patients in my Lafayette practice needing pain management with opioids and certainly saw many patients with Medicaid. But in Thornton about 60-70% of patients I saw required opiates, so I took some continuing medical education classes to learn how to do my job better and more safely. Despite these challenges, I was energized by the racial and cultural diversity in my Thornton patients.

There are many facets to chronic pain and opioid dependence. In pain management, it is imperative that a contract be in force signed by patient and doctor. Such contracts spell out what is expected of the doctor and the patient in the pain management setting. There should be imaging studies or other information that document the likely cause of the patient's ongoing pain. The patient promises to use no more than the prescribed amounts of opioids for each 30 days between office visits, and to fill no other narcotic prescription—even from an ER or a dentist. They know they will have random urine tests that will detect what substances they are taking or not taking. Testing will also show if they are taking any disallowed substances, such as methamphetamine and cocaine. At least a dozen of my patients were dismissed for failing a urine test during my nearly three-year gig in Thornton.

Quite a few patients from my Lafayette practice had followed me to the Thornton practice. They have learned that, as their doctor, I love my job and will do the utmost to provide quality care for any patient I see. Thinking back about patients who had followed me from Longmont to Lafayette, I was reminded of how I had allowed myself to go on "ego trips" about what a wonderful doctor I must be! Then, with unapologetic stoicism, Mrs. Kelly had told me the only reason their family followed me to Lafayette from Longmont was that it was just too damn much hassle to change.

And I continued to find the humor that exists with patient care, no matter where my trade is practiced. A new patient in Thornton, a serious guy in his forties, was seeing me for a physical exam. As part of my exam of the musculoskeletal system, I always test the strength of various movements of the patient's extremities against my resistance. I asked him to pull my arm toward him with his flexed arm against my resistance. Just as we began, he stopped and announced: *Doc, I gotta' tell ya' somethin'!* I was surprised by the interruption. Not trying to sound too boastful he informed me: *"Well, doc, in 1998 I was the*

Colorado state arm-wrestling champion and I just don't wanna' hurt ya'!" That I did not burst out laughing was another aplomb!

After nearly three years in the Thornton practice, I decided to terminate. The main reason was the extreme imbalance of the patient population toward pain management. For me, I'd rather have a balance of patients who are seeing me for wellness and sickness visits.

For most of my adult life, I have been an activist for social justice and health care reform. I have pondered where this activism gene of mine came from. I do think it is related to the non-prejudiced gene that is part of who I am. Perhaps this phenomenon began by choosing my parents wisely. My father interacted with all sorts of people and acknowledged and appreciated diversity. His favorite concert singer was Paul Robeson, an African American basso who was also a great athlete and strong civil rights advocate. As avid baseball fans, Dad and I applauded the appearance of Jackie Robinson in the Major Leagues. My dad, brother and I had the privilege of watching him play at Wrigley Field several times and later witnessed the acquisition of many more talented players of all races. It's about skills and talent, isn't it? Certainly it was not skin color, as my mother had pointed out when I was a child seeing my first "colored person."

When Dad developed tuberculosis of the larynx in the mid-1940s, he was required to go to Oakdale Sanatorium near Iowa City for about a year. Doctors in towns near Elgin volunteered to come to his office on a regular basis to cover his practice. Dad's roommate, Mr. Jim Cotton, whom I mentioned earlier, was African American, the newest, politically correct term.

The author protesting for health care reform in Boulder, Colorado.

Dad regarded him as another human being with TB. Clearly I learned from his example.

In the 1950s a leaflet was issued by the Houston Texas Police Department titled "Twelve Rules for Raising Delinquent Children." It has been reprinted many times and includes recent on-line versions. Some of the rules are: Begin at infancy to give your child everything they want. In this way, the child grows up believing the world owes them something. When they pick up bad words laugh at them. This will make them think they are cute and encourage them to pick up cuter phrases that will blow your mind. Never give spiritual training until they are 21 and let them decide for themselves. Pick up all things they leave laying around the house. Do everything

Howie moderates a panel at the University of Colorado World Affairs Conference, ca. 2003. The Health Reforms panel included social activist Dr. Patch Adams.

for them so they will be experienced in throwing responsibility to someone else. Quarrel frequently in front of your children. Give your child all the spending money they want. And never let them earn their own. Always take your child's side against neighbors, teachers, and police. They are all prejudiced against your child. When they get into trouble apologize for yourself, saying "I never could do anything with them."

My mother saw this piece printed in the *Des Moines Register* and wrote a 13th suggestion which was published in the early 1960s by *Register* columnist John Reynolds: *"Teach your child at an early age to hate anyone whose religious beliefs differ from yours. Don't mingle with people whose skin is a little darker than yours. Instill in your children the idea that people who belong to minority groups have no right to live in our society and it's permissible to bomb and desecrate their houses of worship. If parents can achieve this, they will have taught their children to hate."* Mom was remarkably ahead of her time and her contribution to my DNA undoubtedly nurtured my social justice and activism genes.

Maybe part of that activism spark could have come from Hank Berry during my college days or Clarice Davis, the X-ray technician I befriended during internship in Galveston.

As an activist for serious health care reform, I am a proud member of Healthcare for All Colorado and one of more than 20,000 members of Physicians for a National Health Program. Over the last 40 years, I have written letters to editors, guest opinions, appeared on TV and radio, served on panels, participated in debates, and have given countless presentations to groups. Yes, I have even marched for the cause of universal health reform. So far, I've not been arrested.

A whole treatise could be written about the changes in the practice of medicine over the past 50 years. Evidence shows that state-of-the-art imaging studies, improved prescription drugs, newer immunizations, and surgical techniques have saved millions of lives in our country. What is appalling, however, is that with the United States' health care non-system, access to these remarkable improvements is not available to all our citizens.

Insurance companies use 18-33% of our premiums for purposes other than health care. By contrast, Medicare, a government program, has administrative costs of about 3%. Therefore, many premium dollars sent to insurance companies are not used for health care but rather to pay CEOs' inflated salaries and their golden parachutes when they leave. Of course, there is a need to keep the company profitable for shareholders. Pharmaceutical companies, like health insurance companies, spend a lot of money on advertising, marketing, and lobbying. Medical expenses are the leading cause of personal bankruptcies in our country. More than 50 million Americans lack health insurance and many others are underinsured.

Pharmaceutical companies benefited from a sweet deal delivered in the 2003 Medicare Prescription Drug, Improvement, and Modernization Act. They do not have to negotiate prices. Consequently they can charge Medicare patients much more for medications than they do Veterans Affairs or Medicaid patients or government-run programs in other countries. In my view, lobbyists for insurance and pharmaceutical companies, as well as the lack of meaningful campaign finance reform, are the main obstacles to achieving serious health reform. While the Patient Protection and Affordable Care Act (often called Obamacare) has some shortcomings it could mark the beginning of meaningful change. Reliable surveys have shown that more than 60% of Americans — including more than 50% of physicians — favor a government-run Medicare-for-all program paid for by our taxes. The private insurers and pharmaceutical companies are ripping all of us off: doctors, other providers, hospitals, and patients.

It has always disturbed me that many patients are denied access to basic health care in the U.S. Thousands of Americans die annually because of lack of access, usually for financial reasons. All other industrialized countries except ours consider health care a basic right. Although their systems vary, insurance and pharmaceutical companies are more regulated in other countries, according to *The Healing of America: A Global Quest for Better, Cheaper, and Fairer Health Care* by T. R. Reid (Penguin Press, 2009). Access to care and bankruptcies due to medical bills are not issues in those countries.

Lack of access to care affected one of my favorite patients, but efforts by many people in the community provided a happy ending. Every family doctor has patients they especially enjoy. Bob Carnahan was overweight, diabetic, had heart disease, and liked to smoke cigars, but none of this information helps to describe who he was. He died in 2012 at the age of 85. Our friendship began in the 1970s when Karen's restaurant in downtown Louisville was in its infancy. On most weekdays, Bob and I would have breakfast together and usually flirt with and harass the waitresses, now known as servers. We'd discuss the world's problems and often had the solution to many of them at hand! We worshiped our Denver Broncos through good and bad times, and always had Monday-morning advice we would have given to the various coaches had they only asked.

Bob was a close friend of Karen's, and often in exchange for meals there, he built many of the restaurant's furnishings, including a startling mahogany bar and adjoining cabinets. He was always available to help fix things. The waitresses loved Bob, who was jovial and interactive with all. He was nicknamed "Nice Man Bob."

Bob was a remarkable guy. His talent as a fine woodworker and craftsman was widely recognized. There were many items of furniture in my Lafayette office and my house made by Bob. His range of wordworking projects varied from building quality cabinets and bars to making ornate furniture to putting in doggie doors. He also built a set of shelves for papers in my office lab and racks for charts outside each room. Each of my exam rooms featured a cabinet/desk built by Bob Carnahan. In my house there's a built-in bookcase and a large, gorgeous oak entertainment center. I will never part with this piece.

But, most important, Bob Carnahan loved people and people loved Bob Carnahan. He was a humanitarian with deep concerns for all people. He had overcome many obstacles in his own existence, but never lost his zest for life nor his great sense of humor. That he cared about people and their problems was evident to all who knew him.

Bob had severe hearing and sight impairments which eventually reduced his ability to do his craft. He did not have health insurance and could not afford to have his cataracts removed or to see a specialist about his hearing. I told Bob's story to the CEO of Boulder Memorial Hospital and colleagues representing eye and hearing specialties. The surgery to remove his cataracts and the treatments and devices to improve his hearing were scheduled and done almost gratis, thanks to the benevolence of the hospital and the specialists. Karen and the waitresses held a Sunday brunch with all proceeds — including tips from the 400+ patrons — going to help with incidental costs. Thousands of dollars were raised and Bob was grateful and humbled. "I'd been looking at a pretty dull world," Bob told a reporter from a local paper who covered the story, "but things look so different now." He had done so many favors and built so many things for little or no cost for others, the fans of Bob Carnahan came through. With a tear in his eye he exclaimed: "I wish I could thank everyone personally, but all I can say to everyone is thank you, and you know who you are."

Top: Waitress flirting with Nice Man Bob.
Left: Bob and Karen Mulholland.

Fundraising for local carpenter

Community effort helps restore sight, outlook

By CAMERON LEWIS

"Every time I mention what someone has done for me, they say, don't single me out, think of all the other people who helped." said Bob Carnahan. "So all I can say to everybody is thank you, and you know who you are."

Carnahan has a lot to be thankful for: a month ago a community effort by businesses, doctors, friends, neighbors and strangers all got together to do what they could to help restore Carnahan's sight.

"I'd been looking at a pretty dull world," he said Tuesday, "but things look so different now." Carnahan had successful surgery two weeks ago to correct a cataract and to implant a synthetic lens in one eye.

A self-employed carpenter, Carnahan knew for several years he needed the surgery, but he found himself unable to afford insurance. Other personal, family needs used up the money he'd saved for the operation.

His vision continued to get worse, but Carnahan continued to work, hoping somehow to come up with the money to restore his sight. That somehow turned out to be a community effort.

A local restaurant which is closed on Sundays opened its doors and sold admission to Sunday Brunch. Over 400 people came to eat and proceeds were all donated to Carnahan's medical expenses.

Those who didn't actually come and eat breakfast, which was donated by the restaurant, sent donations of $10, $25, even $100 from a local business. The waitresses, all of whom donated their time that Sunday, encouraged the customers to leave a big tip, and the tips also went to Carnahan's cause.

The breakfast and fundraising covered about half of the necessary expenses, and then two doctors, one in Lafayette and one in Boulder, joined in the spirit. They dropped their fees substantially, including fees for the surgeon who eventually performed the operation. A hospital in Boulder decided with all the effort that had taken place, the administration could cut in half the cost of the hospital stay.

An ear doctor had Carnahan's hearing re-tested

as a service, and discovered there had been a hearing improvement in one ear. Ironically, Carnahan had been wearing his hearing aid in the wrong ear.

"That was a miracle," Carnahan said. "For 38 years, this has been my better ear, and suddenly I can hear in my other one."

But, more than the hearing, Carnahan's outlook has changed along with his improvement in vision. "I don't take anything for granted anymore. I keep wondering 'why me?' Why is all the attention directed at me?" It feels awesome. In order for it to really register, I may have to be hit with a hammer."

What's surprising to Carnahan, on top of everything else, is that so many people contributed. "Over 400 came to the brunch," he said. "I don't know that many people."

Carnahan said he tried to talk his good friend, the owner of the restaurant, out of opening on Sunday. "I told her she needed a day to rest," he recalled, "and if she did open, I wasn't coming down.

But he did go down to the restaurant that Sunday, still a little in the dark about what was going on. "The people were dressed up. A couple of the girls looked real good," he said. "Then one asked me to come into the kitchen to see something. Well, I do some work for them, and I said 'not on Sunday.' But I went into the kitchen, and they told me what this was about."

Carnahan lights up as he recalls what happened next "I had to kiss everyone of them girls,"

he says solemnly.

Carnahan said his decision to come to Louisville 17 years ago turned out to be "a good decision on my part."

The operation turned out to be a success. The day after the operation, Carnahan said his vision was already greatly improved. Now he can see down the street without glasses, and a ceiling which once appeared solid has straight solid lines of tiles. A favorite colorful plaid wool shirtjacket, which Carnahan thought was fading, is beautiful again.

"Look at all that color," Carnahan said, holding it with an expression of seeing again for the first time.

It will be a few months before Carnahan begins working again, but he's already been out to look over some of the work he did before his vision was improved. He's been a carpenter for 25 years, and before that, he says, he was the kid everybody went to when they wanted something built.

"If you wanted a lemonade stand or a tree house, it was 'get Bob,'" he said.

Now the tree houses and lemonade stands of later generations can be appreciated by Carnahan as he takes long walks to the parks, and visits his friends around town.

He still doesn't know what to make of the "pitch-in" effort by so many people, but he appreciated every one of them the moment the doctor took off his bandages and he could see more clearly than he had for years and years.

COMMUNITY EFFORT helped provide cataract surgery to restore the sight of Louisville resident Bob Carnahan. "I'd been looking at a pretty dull world," he says.

"These are Americans. These are good people," he said.

—PHOTO BY CAMERON LEWIS

It should be obvious that other countries have solved the problems of access to care. Their governments struggle with cost control measures at times, but basic health care is not denied to their citizens. Waiting times for elective surgery are often longer than here, but statistics for maternal and neonatal deaths and longevity are better than in the United States. The World Health Organization ranks us 37th in the world in health care, just behind Slovenia! In those countries with some type of universal care, there are fee schedules, rules for payment, and global budgets established by the civil employees who manage these systems.

But in the governments of Europe, Canada, Japan, Taiwan, and Australia, for example, there are not chief executives and other high-ranking corporate officials drawing huge, unconscionable salaries. Nor is there an impetus to do more surgery, sometimes unnecessarily, just to make more money. There have been many reports from various locales in the United States featuring inexplicably higher rates of heart surgeries and hysterectomies compared with similar populations elsewhere. One obvious reason for the disparity is that a high percentage of graduating doctors here must repay student loans of $200,000 or more. In most countries with a national health system, medical education and nursing are highly subsidized by their governments.

Why can't we get the moral fortitude to consider basic health care a right for all and to emulate what we know has worked in other nations for years? Martin Luther King, Jr., said, *"Of all the forms of inequality, injustice in health care is most shocking and inhumane."* In my many years of seeing patients, I can attest as to how correct he really was. Sadly, the situation has not improved and is actually growing worse.

Two of the most egregious examples of health care injustices in our country involved African Americans. From 1932 to 1972 a well-publicized Tuskegee, Alabama, experiment took place. Hundreds of black men, some with and some without syphilis, were studied. Those who had the disease were not told, nor were they treated for it. They just knew they were receiving free health care. The case of Henrietta

Lacks is less well known. This young black mother developed cervical cancer and died before her 40th birthday. Without her knowledge or permission, cells we taken from her rapidly growing tumor in 1951 and have been used around the world as a tissue culture of cancerous cells. The cells, known as HeLa cells, have been utilized for thousands of clinical studies and, according to biology professor Dr. Donald Defler, "They have been among the most important things that have happened in medicine." Yet the surviving family of Henrietta Lacks never received recognition or compensation, although millions of dollars of profits have been made by many people because of those precious cells. Rebecca Skloot recently authored a well-researched book called *The Immortal Life of Henrietta Lacks* (Crown Publishers, 2010).

I did consider looking for part-time work in Boulder, where I live. There was nowhere for me to practice part-time and bring my loyal patients with me, should they chose to follow. I considered applying at the People's Clinic in Boulder. I met with Amy Alper, P.A., for my intake interview and was impressed with the many ways she and others in the Peoples Clinic/Clinica network serve the underserved. These clinics now provide a safety net for so many. She did say that if I really wanted to work at People's or Clinica, it would be hard for them to turn me down since they had long ago named a room after me at Clinica for my efforts to help that organization get started! I did "shadow" a family doc at People's Clinic. I was blown away by how much things had changed and how many thousands of patients are served at the various locations. After considerable thought, I decided not to work there, however, because my Spanish was not as fluent as it needed to be, nor was I eager to learn a whole, new Electronic Medical Record system. I may do some volunteering there in the future.

The practice of medicine includes frustrations and disappointments for sure, as well as the inherent joy. Yet it is clear that there is a human connection—a desire and intent to help someone else, even if healing is not always the end result.

But the "art of medicine" involves more than just seeing patients and making money while doing so. In the altruistic sense, any healing profession is marginalized in the corporate setting. The notions of competing for patients and marketing seem incongruous to a doctor or to anyone who feels that health care should be a right. Yes, this is capitalism at work. I understand the concept that a corporation must make money to survive. But, to me, providing health care is much different than making or selling a product. That is precisely why other industrialized countries have decided that profiteering has no place in delivering quality, basic health care and preventive services to all their citizens.

Under the Affordable Care Act (Obamacare), several significant changes occurred. No longer could insurance companies refuse to cover someone due to a pre-existing condition, nor could they charge more to women than men. Further, there could be no cap on the amount a company must pay, and parents could cover their adult children while in college until age 26. Further, insurance companies were required to spend 80% of premium dollars on health care. Thirty million more Americans were eligible for Medicaid and many others could obtain private insurance. Sadly, there are not enough primary care providers to effectively see all these new patients. Even worse is that referrals of Medicaid patients is fraught with delays and refusal by specialists to accept them or limiting the number seen. Further, Obamacare has left millions of Americans uninsured and underinsured. The high amounts of deductibles have been shown to delay access to care, leading to worse outcomes.

I was hopeful that health care could become more affordable and accessible, but my hopes have diminished since Donald Trump was elected president. Most of all, this country needs a transparent system with accountability, without duplicity, inefficiencies, and the focus on profits. Once and for all, we should emulate those countries that provide excellent health care for less cost while featuring better outcomes. A Medicare for All plan is favored by most Americans and a majority of American doctors, according to published surveys.

I had avoided using the "r" word, since I really didn't want to quit seeing patients nor put to rest those feelings of gratification I had received through the years. But, alas, I decided to retire in July 2016, almost 54 years since joining the Longmont Clinic.

Unapologetically, while growing up I never wanted to become a doctor, but, now that I am, it is clear that the practice of medicine is primarily about the human connection—the desire to heal and comfort others.

Special Thanks

I would like to offer my deepest thanks to Julia Ingalls of Culver City, California, Susan Wortman from Clinica Campesina, and Bill Cameron of Lafayette, Colorado, for their all-important suggestions on how to help with the framework, flow, and the personality of my book. Also, thanks to Michelle Asakawa for her diligent proofreading, and to David Hitchcock for putting my typed words into a real book.

And thanks to my lovely and talented wife for her support and patience with me as I wrote this book.

•   •   •

The Hippocratic Oath, the creed of all physicians, includes:

TO RECKON all who have taught me this art equally dear to me as my parents and in the same spirit and dedication to impart a knowledge of the art of medicine to others. I will continue with diligence to keep abreast of advances in medicine. I will treat without exception all who seek my ministrations, so long as the treatment of others is not compromised thereby, and I will seek the counsel of particularly skilled physicians where indicated for the benefit of my patient.